A Guide for Effective Psychotherapy

John R. Morella, Ph.D.

A Guide for Effective Psychotherapy

For information address:
Helm Publishing
3923 Seward Ave.
Rockford, IL 61108
815-398-4660
www.publishersdrive.com

ISBN 0-9778205-3-X
Printed in the United States of America

Morella, John R., 1941-
A Guide for effective psychotherapy / John R. Morella.
p. cm.
ISBN 0-9778205-3-X (pbk. : alk. paper) 1. Psychotherapy--Popular works. 2. Psychotherapy patients. 3. Consumer education. I. Title.RC480.515.M67 2006
616.89'14--dc22

2006024886

Acknowledgements

My wife, Charlene Webb Morella, has been my soul mate for a long time. Besides caring for our two children and coping with her own work experiences, she has given loving support in my obtainment of graduate degrees, teaching career, starting a clinical practice, and several business ventures. Just when she thought we would rest, I decided to write a book. She was the first to read the manuscript, edit, and as always, offer her support. Thank you, Charlene.

I would also like to thank the many professionals and laypersons who read my work, offered their opinions and contributed much to its refinement. Thank you, guys.

Dianne Helm, C.E.O. of *Helm Publishing Inc.,* has demonstrated patience and guidance. She's truly an author's publisher. Thank you, Dianne.

Table of Contents

Chapter 1 outlines the benefits for the reader who is considering psychological treatment. The millions each year who enter psychotherapy need to have information to make intelligent decisions before therapy. The author's bias toward specific therapy orientations is stated up-front. This book is directed to the layperson, and avoids the scholarly tone, yet presents accurate information.

Mental health providers are many, and have different titles and training. The reader is provided with clear, concise qualifications, training and certification requirements of each of the mental health providers. After reading this chapter, there should be no confusion in the similarities and differences of mental health specialists. The potential client is advised on how to go about determining the qualifications of therapists that best fit their needs. Each of the professionals discussed have overlaps in their training, but the differences in training should be carefully considered by the patient.

Chapter 3 is the longest chapter, and its length is justified. The reader must grasp the basic psychotherapy theories and applications. All therapy approaches are not created equal. The therapy models are explained in a straightforward manner without excessive terminology, language easy to comprehend, and new knowledge that makes sense. "Bullets" are provided to summarize the tenets of each therapy approach. The reader is given an interesting crash course in therapeutic orientations. Using plenty of examples, a maze of therapy theories is made easy to follow.

Comprehensive explanations are provided so the reader can fully appreciate what each therapy format entails. The integration of the therapy orientations with the formats of therapy lends greater clarity to each. Special concerns of couples, group and family therapies are outlined. With the advent of managed care insurance programs, brief therapy is clearly defined and its impact highlighted in a pro/con manner. Play therapy is defined for its appropriateness with children, and its methodology is further elaborated in Chapter 6. The therapist/client alliance in individual therapy provides an advanced look into this unique helping relationship. Valuable insights into group psychotherapy provide an alternate choice for the client.

Chapter 5 incorporates some of the “nuts and bolts” of the psychotherapy process. Specific details of each of the chapter units are explained, providing the reader clarity to clients’ rights. Those who seek therapy need awareness of their equal partnership with the therapist. In order to achieve parity, they require this knowledge prior to stepping through the therapy door.

Chapter 8 provides the reader with the consolidation of the major areas presented in this book. It's a review of what has been presented, set in 13 summarizing paragraphs. I "baled the hay" for the consumer of psychotherapy.

A short list of references is provided directing the reader to further exploration of the major therapy orientations and other areas covered within the book. Comments are added to the referenced books.

A few mental health jokes are sprinkled throughout the book, hopefully provoking a smile or a laugh. Humor is said to be healthy for our physical and psychological well being.

I've provided the reader with numerous resources for educating themselves relative to their disorder, as well as a source for support. Friends and family may also want to avail themselves to the resources listed in this chapter. Support groups have been demonstrated as valuable as the primary therapy regiment.

This ending chapter provides the reader with a "peek" into the therapy room of four actual case vignettes that are "fictionalized" to protect the privacy and confidentiality of the real clients. The purpose of this chapter is to give the reader a more accurate account of what transpires in a therapy session as opposed to how movies, television, novels and plays have depicted psychotherapy. The reader can vicariously experience the realistic therapy process.

Chapter 1: Introduction

Author's Motives for Writing This Book

The purpose of this book is to assist the reader in clarifying what often times can be a confusing, unknowledgeable leap into the murky water of psychotherapy, with its many terms, therapies, and differently trained providers. I've witnessed the apprehensive faces of those who entered the "therapy room" for the first time. While part of the angst they emitted was due to the disorder they came to talk about, the other part of their discomfort was not knowing what to expect. This book was written to help the client know what to expect *before* they walk through the therapy door. Why before? The more information you have prior to entering therapy, the more viable you will be as a client. You can establish a readiness to make decisions on the type of therapy orientation, format of your therapy, and have some sense of how therapies are performed. What I present within these pages takes the mystery out of the therapy process. Life is enough of a puzzle, so you don't need your effort in psychotherapy to be an additional puzzle. Professional psychotherapy is not like what is portrayed on television. Very seldom will you find a goateed therapist, seated behind a reclining client. You generally will not have a repressed memory, when revealed, cures all of your disorders. Therapy has a reasonable process, requires a trained therapist, and most helpful to an effective outcome, a knowledgeable client. After reading my book, you will enter the therapy room with less apprehension of psychotherapy and a sense of management (empowerment) of *your treatment.*

This effort is not intended as a scholarly book, but it presents accurate information. It is based on many years of experience providing psychological services to the public. The book also incorporates hundreds of hours of consultation with other mental health providers, physicians, educators, attorneys, and social agencies. It is a straightforward, direct aide to millions of people who seek psychotherapy every year in our nation. It will contain few references within its paragraphs, no footnotes, and no long list of references at its conclusion. I will recommend a small number of books to those of you whose interests are piqued by the various major theories and applications of psychotherapy (treatment) discussed. This book is written for the layperson that may have had a course or two of psychology in high school or college, or maybe none. He or she may be a secretary, a teacher, a bookkeeper, an attorney, a carpenter, a homemaker or parent, and many other people who have busy lives, and don't have a need to know about psychology, and more specifically, about psychotherapy. Then "life" began to be painful. The "pain" may have come from a host of environmental or internal stressors: a family issue, a child who is distressed and is no longer afforded the joy of childhood, an adolescent who has gone beyond typical teen rebellion, a woman trying to cope with breast cancer, a couple on the brink of divorce, an individual's struggle with sexual identity confusion, a child custody battle, drug abuse, sexual abuse or sexual dysfunction, depression and a host of other human conditions. Perhaps, at this point, psychotherapy became a focus.

How do you know if you need psychotherapy? If you bought this book at your favorite bookstore because it was recommended to you, or perhaps you browsed the "psychology" or "self-improvement" sections, there is a good chance you have considered psychotherapy. You have talked to your family, friends, clergy, physician, and even the friendly bartender, and were unsatisfied with the caring, but direct advice they have given you. They didn't seem to really listen. Or maybe, because they cared about you, they found it difficult to tell you what they really think. Or maybe you couldn't tell them what is troubling you because of fear, embarrassment, or rejection.

Possibly, in the quiet moments in bed at night, waiting for sleep to come, you felt overwhelmed, anxious or depressed, guilt ridden, and unable to cope with your suffering. Unhealthy habits have temporarily numbed you from your suffering. If you are having significant problems in one of the two most important of adult needs, *love* and *work*, the chances are good that you may benefit from therapy. This is a question only you can answer, and it may require you some time to get there. But, you will know when it's time to take care of yourself, and rid the suffering in your life. Trust yourself and also trust the therapist to assist you in determining your need for therapy and establishing clear goals toward healing. Remember your physical health and your mental health are inter-related, and both require attention. Over the many years of my practice, I have consulted with numerous physicians. They related that a significant number of patient complaints and disorders appear to have their origin in unresolved psychological stress and in poor coping skills.

What you will read in this book is a guide toward understanding the following: the various mental health providers available and their training requirements, the major orientations of psychotherapy as well as their supportive theories (as you read the descriptions, ponder which ones make sense to you). You'll need to be familiar with the treatment formats (individual, couples, group, or a combination of these) and play therapy for children. Issues in confidentiality, how to understand your diagnosis, brief therapy and its relationship to managed care insurance, ethics in therapy, and other issues important in the client-therapist alliance are discussed. How to locate referrals and how to interview a perspective therapist is clearly, and in a step-by-step manner, provided. A chapter on children and teens in psychotherapy will assist parents in the process of knowing how to prepare their child, what the therapist will need to know about your child/teen, and what you need to ask the therapist. A section on children and teens on psychiatric medication is explored and a wonderful reference is given to assist parents in this difficult decision. I believe the thoughtful information presented in this book will enhance your opportunity to choose the right therapist.

O. K., let's agree, depending on whom you read, many people have emotional adjustment disorders, or some sort of personality dysfunction, that would require some form of treatment, either with psychotherapy, or medication, or a combination of both. For example, 15 to 20 percent suffer some form of depression. When we add in anxiety disorders and all the other aforementioned disorders, we have a significant percent of our population that may seek psychotherapy. Your friend, family member, your physician, clergy, attorney, etc., may tell you, "Bill, you might want to consider some counseling," and they may even recommend one or a number of therapists. You finally agree. Do you just take one of their recommended names, call and make an appointment? *NO, NO*, and *NO!*

This little book hopefully will assist you in an educated, intelligent process to finding the right psychotherapist. Yes, following my suggestions, may take some time and effort, but you are taking the first step to helping yourself, not to mention the money saved, in having to fire your first, or your second therapist for not helping or you not feeling comfortable with him/her. (For ease of reading, the client/patient will be a "he/ him," and the therapist will be a "she/ her.")

Let's get back to my *"no, no, and no"* exclamation. There are numerous things to consider in choosing a psychotherapist. I'm sure you would spend significant, thoughtful time in selecting a new car, and certainly, in building a house. What's the reputation of the builder, can I work with him in a five to a six-month project harmoniously, and will he be truthful and honest in his dealings with me? Of course you would. Wouldn't you also want to make the same intelligent decision in choosing a therapist? After all, it will represent an important relationship of sharing your deepest thoughts, feelings, and past behaviors that you may not have told any other human. I have had many clients express that the therapeutic relationship was a rare opportunity in their lives where they could cry, express fear, remorse and anger with the unconditional acceptance of their therapist. Something profound happens in the alliance between the client and the therapist. With this said, don't you want to know about the person with whom you will be sharing your very personal issues? It is very important to know what specific training the therapist has, and the level of experience in working with your problem(s). When I had clients, who had prior knowledge of the therapy process, ask good, thoughtful questions about my training, experience, and policies of my practice, I sensed a person who was motivated to make changes in their lives. I was motivated by their desire to seriously participate in this process of change. After all, therapists are human, and benefit from a motivated client. It also keeps the therapist on her toes. Lastly, after you have exercised the knowledge presented in the chapters, your potential for a good therapeutic outcome is enhanced. Therapy is hard work for both parties and this book will assist you in this process.

What is important to understand is that you must want treatment. You must be willing to endure the process with patience, as there is no magic, no quick resolution. Your motivation must be more comprehensive than pleasing your spouse, friend, lover or complying with the recommendations of your physician or attorney. Therapy will be a mutual trusting alliance, regardless of the therapeutic model you choose. "Will power" to change will have little or no impact on your outcome, but a willingness to change is paramount. Giving up neurotic patterns of behavior, irrational thinking, "comfortable," but destructive feelings, are the keys to a healthier life.

As a psychologist licensed by the Louisiana Board of Examiners in Psychology, I was in full time private practice with two other licensed psychologists, and one Board Certified Social Worker (BCSW), for eighteen years. I hold a Ph.D. in Counseling Psychology, and a Master Degree in Special Education. My undergraduate degree is in Psychology. Additionally, I was an academician for sixteen years, at two universities. It is from this background, I draw the information and experience for this book. I hope you benefit.

Author's Bias, Right up Front

Basically, psychotherapy is any psychological approach used to assist positive changes in behavior, personality or in life's adjustments. There are many techniques that have promulgated since the early days of exorcism. Sigmund Freud, through his brilliant development of psychoanalysis, provided the first form of therapy, and since then, numerous other forms have emerged. Most, if not all, psychotherapists have a bias toward one or two major types of therapy orientations that they frame around the client's problems. Obviously, their therapy orientation is a reflection of their training. Yet, many therapists may move away from their early training and make adjustments to their therapy approach. They make the changes with the experiences gained and in evaluating therapy outcomes. Most pursue further training to become proficient in other modalities of therapy orientations. Psychotherapy techniques are many, but a smaller core number of therapy approaches are used among psychologists, psychiatrists, social workers, and other counselors.

As promised, I will disclose my specific bias toward the primary therapy orientations I used with my clients in a *group* practice of psychologists and social workers. I mention group practice, because later in this book, I will elaborate on a solo practice versus a group practice, as it relates to finding the right therapist for you. My initial year in graduate school was in Clinical Psychology, and the therapy orientation that we were taught was psychoanalytic or sometimes called, psychodynamic. This orientation emphasized hidden, internal impulses, desires, and conflict, thus the unconscious is the predominant force that drives our behavior, emotions, and thoughts. The unconscious desires are felt to be influenced or motivated predominately by sexual and aggressive drives. I remember one of my professors saying, "The goal of psychoanalysis is to make the unconscious, conscious." This will be elaborated on later in the book. I left this program, and entered Counseling Psychology. In this program, I was exposed to behavioral and cognitive approaches to altering actions and thoughts, which brought about a subsequent change in feelings. It made sense to me that in behaviorism, one's environment shapes and controls behavior, which is an observable event, as opposed to an unconscious motive, an unobservable event. In cognitive therapy, the focus is on thinking where it is believed that thoughts precede feelings and behavior, thus change the thought and you change the resulting feelings and behavior. A form of cognitive therapy I used frequently, developed by Albert Ellis, Rational Emotive Therapy (RET) will be addressed under the cognitive model of therapy. Many therapists utilize what is referred to as cognitive-behavior therapy, simply utilizing both orientations in treatment approaches (Rational Emotive Behavior Therapy) (REBT). Both therapy orientations are seen as more direct means to alter mental and behavioral disorders in people. Yes, I have seen the value of and have utilized psychoanalytic and humanistic approaches, but I felt it fair to the reader to "put out front" *my strong affiliation to both the behaviorist and cognitive orientations in psychotherapy*. In spite of my bias, I have presented all of the major orientations of psychotherapy, in an accurate and fair manner. With this bias established, let's go on to the important issue of this book, what you should know *before* choosing a psychotherapist.

Chapter 2: Mental Health Providers

Psychologists

Psychologists generally have a doctorate (Ph.D.), (Psy.D.), (Ed.D.) and are trained in methods, knowledge, and theories of psychology. There are numerous specialties in psychology, among them, but not limited to, are clinical, counseling, educational, social, developmental, experimental, school, and industrial organizational. Approximately 60% of all the specialists are in the clinical and counseling areas. These two areas of specialization are specifically trained to diagnose and treat mental disorders, personality disorders, and adjustment problems. Clinical and counseling psychologists have significant training in the assessment of intellectual/cognitive, emotional and personality functioning. Typically three to six years post graduate study is required for the doctorate, and most American Psychological Association approved programs require an internship. In order to call oneself a "psychologist," passing of written and oral examinations by a State Board of Examiners of Psychologists are required, with a period of supervision by a licensed psychologist. Continuing education courses are necessary to maintain the license. Psychologists are not trained or licensed to prescribe medication, but at the time of these writings, two states, New Mexico and Louisiana have adopted or in the process of obtaining limited prescription privileges. Psychologists who pursue this privilege must perform additional schooling, be supervised by a physician (M.D.), and maintain strict guidelines, in order to prescribe.

Psychiatrists

Psychiatrists are medical doctors (M.D.) who specialize in psychiatry. They have completed extensive training in the diagnosis and treatment of mental disorders, and as physicians, are trained to prescribe medications for depression, anxiety, psychosis, and many other mental, neurological and personality disorders. They go to medical school for four years then they receive additional training in psychiatry for three to four years (residency). Psychiatrists are trained in psychotherapy, and may perform both "talk therapy," as well as prescribe medication and monitor medication for other mental health providers who do not have prescription privileges. You may find that psychiatrists who perform psychotherapy, in the absence of medication management, to be few. The "early" psychiatrists were mostly trained in Freudian psychoanalysis, but "today's" psychiatrists perform other forms of psychotherapy. They usually are found in hospital settings and community mental health clinics, while maintaining a private practice. As with psychologists, psychiatrists may specialize in an age group, such as in pediatrics, adolescents, adults, and geriatrics. Frequently, psychologists and other therapists, consult with psychiatrists to prescribe medication for their clients, but still maintain the primary psychotherapy relationship with the client.

Social Workers

Most social workers who provide psychological counseling hold the M.S.W. (Masters of Social Work). Training requires two years of post graduate study and hundreds of hours of "in the field" supervised training. Some may have acquired a doctorate in social work, but typically, those who provide therapy are at the masters' level. They have their own licensing board, have separate autonomy from psychology and psychiatry, and may be found in private practice, schools, hospitals, mental health centers and chemical dependency facilities. They may work closely with psychologists and psychiatrists, performing assessments of family structures, often counseling within the family home. They perform individual, couples therapy, and family therapy. You may also find social workers who go by the titles "psychiatric social workers" or "clinical social workers." Social workers cannot prescribe medications. As with psychologists and psychiatrists, social workers are accountable to their own board of examiners and licensing requirements.

Psychoanalysts

Psychoanalysis refers to a specialized treatment technique or form of therapy that is obtained by further study at accredited programs. Psychoanalysts may be medical doctors, usually psychiatrists, as well as psychologists, and social workers. They obtain a certification in a form of therapy that is associated to S. Freud and his followers. It can best be described as an approach that probes the unconscious mind and its relationship to current feelings, thinking and behaviors. In most instances, part of their training is for the therapist to undergo their own psychoanalysis. Caution should be observed in checking the credentials of anyone identifying themselves as a psychoanalyst. Psychoanalytic therapy is typically of long duration and expensive. To this extent, managed care insurance companies may not cover this form of psychotherapy. You should check with your insurance vendor.

Marriage and Family Counselors, Pastoral Counselors, and Licensed Professional Counselors (LPC)

These titles represent individuals who have at least a master's degree and possibly, a doctorate degree. Most obtain certification and/or license to provide counseling. They treat adjustment disorders in marriage and in the family, and persons requiring supportive therapy. Pastoral counselors have specific training in assisting people who desire counseling in a spiritual framework.

Comments:

First, whoever you choose for a therapist; a psychologist, a psychiatrist, a social worker, a psychoanalyst, or a counselor should hold certification or a license from a state or national board. Additionally, a governing board of her peers should comprise the board of examiners.

Second, most insurance payment plans will only recognize those who hold certification or a license to practice.

Third, check to see if the psychotherapist will work with your age group. For example, some therapists may not work with adolescents, or the elderly.

Fourth, remember, due to different regulations

governing the practice of psychotherapists, just about anyone can call himself or herself a psychotherapist. Always check their credentials.

Lastly, all therapists are not created equal by training.

How about a joke break from all this serious stuff?

> What is the difference between a psychiatrist and a psychologist? If you say to a psychiatrist, "I hate my mother," he will ask, "Why do you say that?" While a psychologist will say, "Thank you for sharing that with us."

Chapter 3: Major Types of Psychotherapy

As you read the following brief descriptions on the schools of thought and methodology of psychotherapy, consider what you believe to be your troubling, psychological issues. The resolution of any disorder may be greatly served by choosing the right therapy orientation. The following descriptions are provided to give you some insight into the different therapy approaches. What I am going to present in this chapter is from many years of experience, and from support of the literature. This is not intended to be a guide as to what therapy model is best suited to a particular psychological disorder, but to give you a starting point, sort of a sense of what seems appropriate for you. *Keep in mind that not all therapy applications are the same.*

Psychoanalytic (psychoanalysis) Model: (Also known as Psychodynamic Therapy)

You may have heard the analogy of the iceberg, the larger part of the iceberg is found below the water surface. To Freud and those psychoanalytic thinkers who followed him, the part that is below the surface is the unconscious, and the smaller part above the surface, is the conscious. In essence, the unconscious has the greater influence on our behavior, thoughts, and feelings. While the unconscious is hidden, and not tangible, it exerts powerful influences on us. The unconscious becomes a depository of repressed memories, those that may cause you significant conflict and anxiety. Most of the conflict, according to this model, arises from drives originating from our primal sexual and aggressive nature. Conflicts in earlier relationships, as with parents, siblings, and others, are evaluated as to its effect in our current lives. These conflicts must be resolved or we are doomed to repeat the same dysfunctional patterns. Most recipients of psychoanalytic therapy are not aware of the multiplicity of hidden conflicts, or the unhealthy defense mechanisms that were utilized. They simply *feel* bad. The role of the therapist in this model is to work with feelings by a number of complex therapeutic methods that probe the unconscious for clues. Through free association (saying whatever comes to mind), and dream interpretation, the therapist seeks the cause(s) through a non-directive therapy approach. Hopefully the patient will gain insights in connecting the unconscious developmental experiences to his current unhealthy feelings and behaviors. Through the insights gained, he begins to test out the new found knowledge in the real world. This model postulates that all behaviors and feelings have their genesis in the past. *The roots of the past must be uprooted, and repotted in the new soil of insight.* As an example of a psychodynamic issue, I remember a very intellectually gifted, adult male client, who presented himself for therapy because he was not able to keep a job for very long. This was in spite of his highly qualified training in his professional field. Job after job, he would end up in telling his supervisor, in unpleasant language, 'to take the job and shove it." He claimed when his boss would criticize some aspect of his work, even in a minor way, he would feel anger, humiliation, unworthiness, and great despair. He said he did not understand his motive for acting and feeling this way. He was worried about the employment record he was creating and the stress it was causing in his marriage, and on his finances. We began to explore his relationship with his parents. Both who were still living, far off in another state. He described his mother as passive, but very nurturing to him and his siblings. She invested her energies in her children, and "we became her life." His father was described as demanding, critical of him, his siblings and his mom. "Nothing was ever good enough for him. We didn't cut the grass right, didn't get enough hits in baseball, or make the grades he demanded. My mom wouldn't stand up to him, for us or herself." As he explored these memories and the feelings of helplessness still stored within him, he began to relate his father to his bosses and their position of power and authority over him. He began to see the relationship of striking out at his supervisors, as striking out at his dad, when he perceived them as critical. Once he made the connection of the unresolved past issue to his current relationships, he was able to make progress on this issue.

I mentioned the non-directive approach used in psychoanalysis. The essence of this approach is that the patient chooses the subject contents, not the therapist. The premise of encouraging the patient to direct the subject matter choices is the assumption that the contents of the patient's utterances are unconsciously generated. The emotional tone in which the experience is expressed is of equal significance with its content. The content produced by the patient is important, regardless of how it may appear at the moment. Patience by the parties in this non-directive approach is paramount, as it may be months or years before significance is obtained.

The psychoanalytic therapist is always aware that the patient's symptoms, whether it is depression, anxiety, eating disorder, or a large number of other disorders, represents some past developmental dynamic, and when uncovered, will ultimately explain the symptoms. This is a cardinal tenet of this model. In addition, Freud proposed that a majority of an individual's personality develops before the age of six and changes minimally thereafter.

If you are seeking advice, direct counsel, and value clarification, you may be very disappointed with the psychoanalytic model as a choice. Psychoanalysts are trained to avoid any direct effort to provide information of these natures, and will resist giving direct advice. There will be an emphasis on you making choices, not the therapist.

It is not the intent of this book, to provide you with the full measure of the therapy rational, techniques and procedures of each therapeutic model. For example, your knowledge of id, ego, and superego concepts will not add much to your choice of a therapist. Knowing about the concept of transference, either positive or negative will not enhance your therapeutic experience. Listing, and explaining the brilliant work of Freud's defense mechanisms, may not assist you in recognizing your own defenses. Knowing the psychosexual stages of development (oral, anal, phallic, latent and genital), will not heighten your recovery from obsessive or compulsive disorders. What is important to communicate to you are the distinct "flavors" of the various therapy models.

Below are listed some of what we have noted as distinct tenets of the psychoanalytic model.

- The unconscious mind has the greater influence on our personality and emotional development than the conscious mind.
- Termed a "deterministic model," meaning that our behaviors, thoughts, and feelings are determined by causes hidden deep within the unconscious, and due to its threatening content, is repressed. The concept of "free-will" is not recognized in this model.
- Psychoanalysis, generally a lengthy process of psychotherapy, explores the unconscious to reveal conflicts mostly of sexual and aggressive origins.
- The client will do most of the talking through free-associating, reporting on dreams, and focusing on the importance of past relationships and its effect on current relationships.
- It's a stage theory, where one must successfully negotiate each stage without becoming stuck (fixated) because of too little or too much stimulation, (under or over-gratification) such as in Freud's psychosexual stage of development. You may have heard of someone having an "oral personality."
- Your relationship with your analyst is

viewed as a mirror of how you manage other relationships in your present life. In essence, psychoanalysis strives to make the unconscious, conscious, which will lead to awareness (insight), and the relief from painful symptoms, both emotional and physical. In other words, what you don't know or don't have awareness of, can hurt you.

- Therapy may be several days a week, or years in duration, but more contemporary analysts utilize "briefer" therapy, in number of sessions and duration. It is still considered the most expensive and time-consuming therapy model.

Even if a therapist is not a psychoanalyst by training, most psychologists, psychiatrists, social workers, and counselors are generally familiar with this model. I have on many occasions utilized some tenets of the psychoanalytic approach in order to treat client dysfunctions. In most cases it was very effective in helping the client form significant insights in the resolution of a disorder.

> "After twelve years of therapy, my psychiatrist said something to me that brought tears to my eyes, "No hablo ingles."
>
> Judy Brown

We are on a roll:

Behaviorist Model

Just as S. Freud is the guru of the psychoanalytic model, John B.Watson is the guru of behaviorism. Developed in the 1930's, by Watson and E. Thorndike, whose mantra was, "enough of studying what people feel and think, let's start studying what people do." In essence, let's deal with overt, observable, tangible, and measurable behaviors, not covert (hidden) emotions, and thoughts. Then in the 1950's, B. F. Skinner took the concepts of Watson and Thorndike, and gave them application to a variety of settings; schools, military, business, and psychotherapy. As a "strict" behaviorist, Skinner constructed many experiments with rats, pigeons, and people that demonstrated the modification of behavior. He did not concern himself with changing thoughts and feelings, which cannot be observed. This was in the belief that if you modify or extinguish destructive and abnormal behaviors, the organism will adjust his thoughts and feelings consistent to more appropriate, functional, newly learned behavior. This view of managing behavior is based on the concept of *operant learning*, in that; one's environment *operates* on the person's behavior.

Obviously, one quickly surmises that behaviorism focuses on the conscious state of the person, not the unconscious state. It also deals primarily with the present and is only interested in the past of the client to establish what dysfunctional behaviors may have been reinforced by the primary caretakers. But, the behaviorist therapist *does not dwell on the past,* historical dynamics of relationships in the client's life. Dreams, unconscious repressed memories, and transference are not in the psychotherapy ballpark of the behaviorist. The psychotherapist will do most of the talking or at least the same amount as the client, and perform a teaching role, outlining the principles of the model.

One of the major tenets of the behaviorist model is the belief that abnormal behavior is learned and can be unlearned, then replaced with more functional, appropriate behavior. When the new behavior exhibits itself, others in his environment will further reinforce the desired behavior. Additionally, the client will feel better as a result of positive reinforcements received within meaningful relationships. He will also think more appropriately without the angst produced by the dysfunctional behavioral patterns

In essence, all behaviors that are followed by a positive consequence increase in frequency, and all behaviors that receive no positive consequence, or an aversive stimulus, decrease in frequency. So how does this relate to a therapy issue? If a client clearly manifests a histrionic personality disorder, and receives attention or affection, for the tearful, seductive behaviors exhibited, the probability of the behaviors noted, will increase, or stay at its high frequency. If a child receives attention, even negative attention, say a scolding for misbehavior, the undesirable behavior will increase in the future. Inappropriate behavior or neurotic behavior can be ignored, or presented with a mildly noxious stimulus. When the person behaves appropriately, positive-reinforcement is presented to increase the frequency of the desired behavior.

Let's examine behaviorism from this following view. A student in a high school chemistry class is paying attention to the teacher, taking notes, and asking questions. These may be viewed as appropriate student behaviors. Other potential options in the student's behavioral repertoire are doodling, yawning, sleeping at his desk, or any number of other "inappropriate" classroom behaviors. Let's further observe that he maintains a high grade point average, receives positive strokes from his teachers and parents, and recognizes a long term gratification of getting into a major university of his choice. Thus, appropriate student behavior in the classroom has been reinforced, and the student directly or indirectly benefits, and will likely continue the appropriate classroom behaviors. The environment operates on this behavior, and strengthens it.

The behaviorist model is also deterministic. A person's behaviors simple or complex are determined by how the environment operates on the behavior, by reinforcing it, ignoring it, or punishing it. The concept of "free-will," in terms of a person actively making choices, is not accepted by the strict behaviorist.

Behaviorist psychotherapists have a large number of techniques that are used in therapy, and outside of the therapy office. Without examining each one, let me just note them so that recognition is established. Among them, are behavior modification, shaping, systematic desensitization, reciprocal inhibitions, in vivo exposure, and modeling, to name a few.

There is usually plenty of "therapy homework," with this model. The techniques taught are practiced within and outside of the therapy room. It may involve charting of behaviors, frequency counts, reading on basic behavior modification models, writing behavior contracts for a dysfunctional child, adolescent or a family. It is a very active, directive, and structured therapy.

Some professional therapists and some clients have expressed criticism toward this model. It is believed to be void of volitional actions, autonomy of the individual is not fostered, and there is an over-deterministic view of man as simply a consequence of classical and operant conditioning. One can imagine when classical Freudian psychoanalysts and strict Skinnerian behaviorists are in the same room, a defined animosity prevails.

Let's do some "bullets" to sum up the behaviorism points of view:

- Behaviorism explores conscious behavior (overt) which can be seen, measured, and modified. The unconscious, dream interpretation, or any forms of altered states of consciousness are not recognized in theory or in application of behavioral therapy.
- All behavior is learned, and can be unlearned.
- Behavioral psychotherapy focuses on the present behaviors of the client. Historical queries into the past are only accomplished to determine how inappropriate or dysfunctional behaviors were initially established and reinforced. The rest of the puzzle is simple. What is learned, can be modified.
- Relative to feelings, behaviorists believe we will feel a positive emotion when our learned behaviors elicit attention, affection, and approval from significant others in our environment.

- Behaviorism has a deterministic bent to it. Our behavior is determined by the present environmental forces acting upon our behavior, whether it is positively reinforced, ignored or receives some form of aversive treatment.
- Autonomy, that is, personal independency, self actualization, and "free will" choices are not entertained in behavioral psychotherapy.
- Behavioral therapy is directive, active, often requiring out-of-the-therapy room activities, (home work). The therapist often assumes a teaching role, with the client as student.
- Behavioral therapy can be used readily with children, adolescents, adults, couples, and groups. Many of the principles of operant learning are utilized in schools, in inpatient facilities, business/industry, and the military.
- Many problems of the client can be addressed in a brief therapy format. Thus, it is viewed as cost effective, compatible with brief therapy and managed care insurance plans. Specific therapy goals are usually set up in the first few sessions.

Cognitive Psychotherapy

The Greek philosopher, Epictetus (c.55-c135), among his many teachings, stated:

"If you are distressed by any external thing, it is not this thing which disturbs you, but your own judgment about it. And it is in your power to wipe out that judgment now."

"It is not what happens to you, but how you react to it that matters."

"Men are disturbed not by things, but by the view which they take of them."

To the cognitive therapist, what you think is what you feel. Thinking always precedes feeling. You don't have a feeling until you have a thought. In order to change the feeling, and the subsequent behavior, you challenge the thought, change it to a more rational one, and you will be less distressed. This is what Epictetus taught many centuries ago.

Two psychologists currently associated with cognitive psychotherapy are Aaron Beck, the developer of the cognitive treatment approach, and Albert Ellis, the creator of Rational Emotive-Behavior Therapy (RET). Both came from a psychoanalytic background, but changed to the belief that cognitive distortions were predominate in mental disorders, notably in depressive and anxiety dysfunctions.

In cognitive therapy, feelings and behavior are also given status, but the major tenet is the examination of the thinking process, as to its rational or irrational content. Human thinking is a representation of what people say, like, “I’m a terrible person for the way I treated my wife,” to sub-vocal or silent thoughts, such as thinking privately, “I will never find someone to love.” Catastrophic thinking is common in all of us, and produces catastrophic feelings. A good clue to whether you have thought catastrophe, is when your language (representative of your thinking) or private thoughts contain, “always,” “never,” “must,” “better,” or “should,” and other demanding words and thoughts. “I must be perfect in all that I do”, or “I am worthless if I am not loved,” or “It’s awful if I don’t get my way.” Ellis has identified hundreds of irrational belief systems that foster neurosis. The RET therapists will challenge (sometimes aggressively, sometimes with humor, and sometimes with debate) the client’s irrational thinking process. Therefore, when a client states, “I will die if my wife leaves me, I just couldn’t go on without her,” the therapist will encourage the client to substitute a more reasonable and rational thinking process with, “It may be unpleasant, inconvenient and unfortunate if your wife wants out of the marriage, but not catastrophic. You are upsetting yourself by believing your world will end with her departure. People don’t die when a divorce happens to them, and neither will you. Try saying and thinking that a divorce will be unfortunate, or unpleasant. What evidence do you have that you could not survive a divorce? Tell me." The therapist will continue to reduce the catastrophic thinking by explaining that outside events do not cause our emotional disturbance, but how we cognitively structure the event does. If "A" is the **a**ctivating event (divorce), "B" is our **b**elief system, ("This is horrible to be happening to me!") ,"C" is the **c**onsequence in feelings or behavior (depression, anger), "D" is **d**isputing of the irrational belief, and "E" is the new **e**ffect where "E" replaces "C", with more rational consequences.. The therapist will dispute and challenge the irrational catastrophic thinking, and assist in replacing it with more rational thoughts.

One of the tasks I would give my clients is simply to discontinue to use catastrophic words, and to demonstrate that words have powers that directly influence our feelings. Such as, "It was *awful* the way my husband treated me on my birthday." I would suggest she try thinking, and saying, "It was *unfortunate* he forgot my birthday this year, but it's not the end of the world." Yes, words we choose to express our emotions have significant power, and when we ruminate, (repeat the same thought over and over) we enhance the impact of the catastrophic feeling associated with the word. If she continues to think it was *awful*, she will most probably treat him (behave) as having done an *awful* thing, and he should be hung from a rope!

Where do we learn our irrational belief systems? Perhaps you learned from your parents, authorities, religion, and other societal agencies. You have been made to feel awful, terrible, worthless, if you commit a human fallibility. You are not a SOB, but a F.H.B., a **F**allible **H**uman **B**eing. While it is important to take responsibility for one's actions and to make amends if we have violated someone's rights, we don't have to perceive ourselves as totally worthless to do so. Assertive skill training is frequently taught to assist people to stand up for their rights, without angry, or violating the rights of the other person. We don't have to upset ourselves, or have anger to be assertive. Inappropriate anger and rage displayed as disruptive and irrational feelings and behaviors are commonly treated in the therapist's office. The anger and rage can be overly significant or minor experiences in our lives. What follows are examples of how anger/rage is ignited by our irrational thinking. If the driver of the first car in line at the red light is talking on his cell phone, and he doesn't step on the accelerator (as light changes to green) when he *should, ought, or better,* and if you (driving the car behind him) become enraged, you are upsetting yourself by thinking he ought to be paying attention and by saying "I *can't stand it!"* Remember, nothing ought, better or should exist, except perhaps in a perfect world. If your brilliant child is making failing grades, and you think, "*This is awful, and I won't allow it,*" these irrational thoughts will quickly lead to irrational feelings and behaviors. And, it all started with a thought! O.K.,

I think you're getting the newest flavor of cognitive therapy. Did you notice my positive bias toward this therapy approach? Remember, I warned you.

Cognitive-Behavioral Therapy is the wedding of both theories and therapeutic processes. Examining and assisting the client with his irrational thinking, and modifying inappropriate self-defeating observable behaviors, can readily be accomplished together. Essentially, we think, we feel, we behave. A cognitive-behavioral therapist can modify any or all, of these three human processes.

Ready for some more bullets. Below are some of the features of cognitive psychotherapy.

- Cognitive therapy asserts we get ourselves into emotional trouble by faulty thinking, or more technically stated, by the irrational beliefs we held and taught to us by a variety of sources.
- There is no effort made by the cognitive therapist to explore the unconscious mind, or associate past experiences to present thinking distortions. Irrational beliefs are learned.
- Cognitive therapy, and certainly behavioral therapy need not explore or confirm the cause of a dysfunction in order to effect cognitive or behavioral change.
- Therapy is active and structured with the therapist in a teaching/guidance role.

Don't be surprised to find yourself in role play.

The client should expect homework tasks that will reinforce the session lessons. (I provided my clients audio tapes produced by A. Beck, E. Ellis and Robert Harper on Cognitive Therapy, RET, and REBT (Rational Emotive Behavior Therapy). Ask your therapist if tapes are available for you. My clients found them helpful.)

- Generally, after the initial few sessions, mutually agreed upon therapy goals will be established.
- The client's choice of words used to express his thoughts will be challenged and debated by the therapist, in respectful, but in a direct manner, sometimes using humor to buffer the confrontations.
- Usually, a brief therapy regiment is sufficient to meet therapy goals. (I frequently schedule a follow-up session about a month or so after the "termination session," to see how the client is maintaining the learned lessons.)

Humanistic Psychotherapy

You may recall psychoanalytic and behaviorism were defined as "deterministic" models, implying that we are governed by forces not in our control or awareness. With the psychoanalytic model, this force was the unconscious, and with the behaviorist model, our environment. The humanistic model rejects the concept of determinism. Humanism stresses "free-will" or the belief that we possess the ability to make choices. Abraham Maslow, and Carl Rogers, are two pioneers in the humanistic approach. They propose a view of mankind that is more positive, seeking to focus on our potential for creativity, finding meaningfulness to our lives, and spirituality rather than pathology (illness). Rogers and Maslow professed keen interests in what makes people psychologically healthy, and those factors that contribute to what Maslow called the "self-actualized" person, an effort that continues throughout life. Briefly, listed below are the characteristics (not in any order of importance) of self-actualization or the fully functioning.

- an acceptance of self and others, an effective view of reality, that is void of dishonesty,
- task and goal directed that goes beyond one's self (community service),
- which lends itself to a deep connection to all humans, and the trials we all share,
- a sense of autonomy, which frees us from dependency on others and authority groups,
- a sense of humor that does not contain hostility toward racial, gender, or ethnic persons,
- the ability to be alone with one's self without feeling alone,
- whether it is a sunset or the birth of a

child, the self-actualized person does not grow tired of appreciating life and maintains a fresh viewpoint of life,

- ability to have what Maslow called "peak experiences," those experiences that bring joy, harmony, and meaningfulness to their lives,
- they are spontaneous, and their thoughts and impulses are not tethered by convention, and are actively engaged in life,
- "self-actualizers" don't procrastinate--they respond with action.

In addition, Maslow felt that it took at least four decades of living to achieve the self-actualized state. In terms of historical figures, some of the people that Maslow felt possessed the above traits were, Gandhi, Abe Lincoln, Albert Einstein, Martin Luther King, Jr., Albert Schweitzer, and Walt Whitman. Maslow's work represents a refreshing view to the nature of mankind.

Let's note what Carl Rogers brought to the *application* of the humanistic-existential model. I have just introduced the word, "existential." Let's introduce another term, "phenomenological." Gee, I'm not sure if I can, in an understandable manner explain these terms, as they relate to Roger's Humanistic Therapy. The latter term first. According to this theory, we all exist in our own interpretation of reality. We relate to what our individual senses allow us to interpret, as we form a subjective point of view. *My phenomenal interpretation of reality is different from yours. So if you want to understand me, you must be able to enter my phenomenal field of reference.* If I am suffering from depression, it would be important for the therapist to be able to enter my idiosyncratic thoughts, feelings, and perceptions of my reality. Does that make sense? Let's try this. Because we exist (existential), we all experience the pangs of despair, anxiety, loneliness and isolation. After all, we are the only "creatures" that have the awareness that we will die. That produces existential anxiety, but we all may perceive this quite differently. So, my humanistic therapist needs to approach me from my phenomenal view-point if she is going to assist me with my emotional pain. How do Rogers and other therapists who embrace this theory go about helping me? Well, he must form a healthy alliance with the client based on mutual trust, honesty, and unconditional acceptance of my phenomenal interpretation of my "existential world." That would include my feelings, thoughts and behaviors. Again, how does that happen? Rogers calls his humanistic therapy, "client-centered therapy." The therapist allows the client to direct the therapy, but under the wings of a compassionate therapist who will guide the client to take responsibility of the choices he made in his life. The present, as oppose to the past, is the timeframe that the client is encouraged to accept. There will be a strong concentration on the subjective feelings of the client, and on-going attempts to enter the phenomenal life-space of the client. As a client relates a subjective feeling or thought, the therapists will confirm he listened, he heard, he made no judgment, accepted the perception, and will often, repeat what the client expressed. "You feel anger toward your wife for not supporting your career change." The client hearing his own thoughts, and feeling replayed by the therapist, gains acceptance of his unique, but valued self. The cornerstones of client-centered or Rogerian Therapy are empathy, unconditional positive regard and acceptance. This environment, in and of itself, is conducive for the client to find his own answers, to untangle his own web of meaningfulness in his life. They have choices to make, and take responsibility for the choices. You don't need psychological testing or diagnosis to do this.

To the humanist, making a diagnosis and aiming the treatment toward the diagnosis may be counter productive. No special therapy techniques are employed, such as you found in the three previous therapies discussed. The relationship between the client and therapist is the key toward a congruent self-concept, a growing awareness of self, and a march toward self-actualization. Therapy can be brief (weeks) or longer (years), and usually at the longer end. Dealing with the larger philosophical issues of life similarity takes more time, plus the client directs the tempo of therapy.

I hope you gained an understandable glimpse of humanistic therapy, and its existential/phenomenal theoretical bent. I know it was difficult for me to find the words to explain its very amorphous structure.

Are you ready for some more bullets that highlight Humanism?

- The basic tenet or premise of humanism is the subjective interpretations that the client brings to therapy. Their phenomenological "life space" is expressed in their feeling, thoughts and behaviors.
- The therapy focuses on the present, not the past of the client.
- It is considered non-direct therapy, in that the client orchestrates the content, speed, and direction of the therapy. However, the therapist has an overall concept of the direction of the therapy. In this regard, it is not so different from psychoanalytic therapy.
- There is a sense of whom we are (self), and a desire for what we want to be (ideal self), and the greater the congruence or agreement between the two selves, the healthier we are.
- The client-therapist relationship is crucial and is characterized by an honest, empathetic, deeply caring, and

unconditional acceptance of the client, conditions that must exist for healthy growth.

- There is a gestalt (whole) approach to treatment of the client's subjective anguish; by that it is meant, the parts of the existential pain are not broken up into parts and treated, because a good therapy outcome results in a healthier integrated whole.
- Major personality change is not a goal of the humanistic approach.
- Psychological testing and diagnosis are not crucial to the treatment process.
- Therapy is usually long-term, in number of sessions, and may be a year or more in duration. The therapist wears no "mask" of authority. She is real, open, and willing to offer empathic listening, and never makes choices for the client. Clients will go in the direction of growth when given the climate to solve their own problems.

No, we are not quite through with the existential stuff. There's another form of therapy application called *Gestalt Therapy*. (At this point, let me mention, almost in an apologetic fashion, there are many, many more psychotherapy approaches we will not discuss. There is Transactional Therapy, Interpersonal Therapy, Adlerian Therapy, Eye Movement Desensitization and Reprocessing Therapy, Logotherapy, etc., and many, many more specific methodologies such as, art/dance therapy, hypnosis, biofeedback, regressive therapy, etc, etc, and etc.. My goal is to provide you with a book that will be a self-contained, comprehensive guide, not an exhaustive one, and stick to the *major forms of psychotherapy orientations*.)

But, I digress. Back to Gestalt therapy which was principally developed by Fritz Perls. Remember, Gestalt, translated means "whole or complete." When perceptions and awareness of self, are disjointed, unfinished, or not connected, we experience a roadblock in our personal growth potential. When we have fragmented experiences, such as unresolved grief for a deceased parent, or not expressing anger and hurt as a victim toward a sexual predator, our feelings and awareness are hindered by fear. This lack of full expression stifles our personal development. Your "here and now" suffers. I have used the gestalt technique, called the "empty chair," to assist clients in coming to grip with "unfinished business" in their lives. Using an empty chair, I will direct a client to visualize his father sitting there and to verbally express to the empty chair, his feeling about his father's chronic alcoholism during his childhood. The result is a resolution of the unfinished business, and the removal of an emotional barrier. Gestaltists believe that people think too much at times, intellectualize too much at times, in attempts to avoid feeling and gaining awareness. How a person says something (mannerisms, inflections, postures, etc.) are perhaps more important data than what they say. Gestalt therapy also has a kinship to the psychoanalytic model. However, it does not focus on the past but on the present. Reality exits only in the present. Confrontation and challenging of the client are a part of the Gestalt therapy experience. When all of the fragmented parts of clients are allowed to find their wholeness ("the whole is greater than the sum of its parts"), their personal awareness is enhanced. Any change that result, is not directed toward some model of healthiness, but to whom you really are---- you.

The Eclectic Therapy Approach

I wasn't quite sure where to place the eclectic approach, as it's not a self-contained theory in psychotherapy. My computer's dictionary defines "eclectic," as "deriving ideas from a broad and varied range of sources." In the context of this book, simply said, a therapist may choose to weave all the above approaches together to match the client's needs, and particular problem(s). It is estimated that fifty percent of therapists utilize an eclectic approach with their clients. There have been many occasions with clients where I've used behavioral therapy, along with a psycho-dynamic approach when I believed the client's past was relative to the present dysfunctions. There can be situations where a therapist may begin in a psychoanalytic mode, and blend in cognitive-behavioral models. In the eclectic approach, the therapist takes clues from the client's irrational thinking, the behavioral patterns that are being reinforced, and "unfinished business", and fragmented feelings, requiring a "Gestalt moment." Borrowing from all the major schools of thought to help the client with his individual needs demonstrates flexibility on the part of the therapist. Let's note one more reason for the value of the elective approach and then we will move onto the next section of the book. Psychotherapy, for the most part, is "talk therapy." This implies verbal skills. Clients come with all levels of verbal skills, from the highly articulate, to the quiet, monosyllable client. For the latter, the more direct, didactic (teaching) styles of therapies seem to be more suitable.

O.K., let's move on----to another joke.

Joe has been seeing a psychoanalyst for four years for treatment of the fear that he had monsters under his bed. It had been years since he had a good night's sleep. Furthermore, his progress was very poor, and he knew it. So, one day he stops seeing the analyst and decides to try something different. A few weeks later, Joe's former psychoanalyst meets his old client in the supermarket, and is surprised to find him looking well rested, energetic, and cheerful.
"Doc!" Joe says, "It's amazing! I'm cured!"
"That's great news!" the analyst says, "You seem to be doing much better. How?"
"I went to see another doctor," Joe says, "and he cured me in one session!"
"One?" the analyst asks incredulously.
"Yeah," continues Joe, "my new doctor is a behaviorist."
"A behaviorist?" the psychoanalyst asks. "How did he cure you in one session?"
"Oh, easy," says Joe. "He told me to cut the legs off my bed."

Chapter 4: Formats for Psychotherapy

Up to this point you have been provided an explanation of the types of psychotherapists, and their training backgrounds, and degrees required for therapists to utilize their profession titles. Additionally, you have been exposed to various major theoretical orientations of mental health therapies. A reminder: Not all psychotherapists are trained the same, thus, all are not "created equal." The same can be said for the theories that support the delivery of therapy. While, there may be some minor overlap in these orientations of therapy, they are distinct models. Also remember, most therapists are trained in several of the major orientations, and can provide an eclectic model, which can blend the formats in helping the client.

Now, let's "discuss" the formats of psychotherapy.

Individual Psychotherapy:

Simply put, one client to one therapist. Individual therapy is the most common format, and as alluded to earlier in this book, the client-therapy alliance within this format may become one of the most intense, emotionally intimate, and extraordinary relationship in the client's past or present. A relationship between friends, husband and wife, or clergy to a parishioner may not be as profound as the individual therapy format. You may be thinking, "The author may be getting a teeny bit melodramatic with that last statement." Not really. Let me explain. A trust will develop (and if it doesn't, fire your therapist), plus mutual respect. The trust and respect allow the client to risk disclosure of thoughts, feelings, and behaviors of the past that may not have been shared with another human being. Acceptance by the therapist is unconditional and without judgment. How often have you experienced unconditional acceptance in two human-beings accepting the fragile nature of their humanity. One is trying to cope, the other trying to help, and both are giving something of themselves.

In psychoanalytic and humanistic models one can readily expect the one-to-one therapy relationship to be crucial to the therapy processes. The personality of the therapist is also perhaps slightly more central to the tenets of psychoanalysis and humanistic models. Why? The client is expected to share, reveal, and emote, and the therapist is to listen. He can't accomplish this with any apprehension of the therapist's feelings. The therapist must have the demeanor of encouraging disclosure, without the client expecting the therapist to respond as their friend, lover or priest. These therapists must maintain a blank slate, yet assuring the clients that their best interests are the central focus. The therapist is there for the client, and it is not a reciprocal relationship. "In the world of psychotherapy, where no sin is recognized, one neither hates nor loves either the actor or the act. Here is a confessional that leads to absolution without penance." (Willard Gaylin, M.D., pg.215)

In cognitive and behavioral models, the client-therapist relationship via individual therapy is also important, but takes on more of a teacher-to-student relationship. The therapist teaches, challenges, refutes, and gives homework, and more of an authority relationship is established. However, trust, rapport, and respect are always present. There may be some sharing by the therapist relative to his own experiences in life, and the coping techniques utilized to resolve problematic issues. I have on occasion, told clients to view me as a teacher, and them as students, not a client or patient. My role was to impart the strategies of cognitive or behavioral principles for them to learn and apply to their emotional, altitudinal, or behavioral problems.

Couples Psychotherapy

As I reflect on my years in practice, in respect to "couples psychotherapy, "I recall those experiences with couples as, "it was the best of times, and the worst of times." By this it is meant, I found couples therapy to be demanding in attempts to maintain the psychological interests of two unique personalities, often expressing their needs, polarities apart. It can also be very satisfying to all parties involved, when the couple's issues were resolved. In this therapy alliance, we have two clients, and obviously, one therapist. The couple pairings may be spouses, lovers living together, (heterosexual or homosexual), and pre-marital counseling. There are couples who have already decided to divorce and desire counsel to reduce emotional scars, particularly when children are involved. There are boss and employer, and isolated other couple pairings who seek therapy. Couples therapy is indicated when there are relationship issues that impact upon a couple's compatibility.

Several interesting observations need to be shared at this point. One member of the couple, at different times, and on different issues, may sense feeling “ganged-up on,” implying the spouse and the therapist are “critical” of him/her. I, as a *male* therapist, working with a male/female couple, have also encountered a “gender issue.” This is when the female spouse believes that the two males are siding with each other on an issue. I remember on one occasion, one female spouse saying in frustration, “there is too much testosterone in this room.” I guess if the therapist is female, there could be a statement of “too much estrogen in this room.” One of the other slippery slopes the therapist must negotiate is to assist the couple in problem solving (a mutual goal) while addressing the individual dysfunction(s) within each of the spouses. To this extent, don’t be surprised if the therapist requests an individual session with one or the other spouse. Sometimes certain childhood issues may need to be addressed in one spouse, which will mandate individual sessions. With married couples or couples living together, among the numerous issues that require amelioration, financial stressors have risen up the list. The current Zeitgeist (spirit of the times) with both spouses working, therapists also witness stress and fatigue issues, division of child care and household chores conflicts, lack of intimacy, all which tax the relationship. On occasions, when there were multiple, intense issues in the couple relationships, I included an additional therapist to assist with the complex dynamics. In all cases, I introduced a therapist who was female to achieve a gender balance.

Relative to the therapeutic orientation applied, couples-therapy may be active, directive and structured. I, based on my admitted bias, find that couples tend to respond effectively to direct and structured models in changing dysfunctional patterns in their relationship.

Group Psychotherapy

Group therapy is a most effective format for many psychological disorders. In may be used in conjunction with individual therapy. Group therapy is no longer viewed as a “step-child” of therapy formats. As the name connotes, group therapy is a group of clients with one or more therapists. Groups may be homogeneous (similar) or heterogeneous (dissimilar) in gender, diagnoses, and age, (child, adolescent, adult). Group size may vary, but I prefer groups no larger than fifteen. Group participation is less costly than individual therapy.

Initially most people have significant reservations and apprehensions about joining a group, on several levels. They perceive that their issues will not be resolved in a group, as they would be in individual therapy, because of not receiving the one-to-one attention and focus. They also hypothesize that talking about their problems to one individual therapist is difficult enough, sharing with a group may be overwhelming for them.

Additionally, they are concerned about confidentiality. All are reasonable concerns. Potential group therapy clients should be provided general information on how group psychotherapy operates, such as, if you prefer not to talk or contribute, and just listen, that's okay, safeguards of confidentially are explained, and other guidelines are set up by the group with input by all members.

When there is a hesitant client, say a adult male, with a complaint/diagnosis of depression, and there is availability of a homogeneous group of depressives, heterogenous in gender and age (young adults-to-geriatric), I then ask that he consider a trial period of a set number of sessions. He has the understanding that he can leave the group and return to individual sessions. Once attending, most clients begin to understand and appreciate the benefits of group therapy. One of the immediate benefits recognized is the fact that they are not alone in their despair, as others express similar struggles and experiences. They are privy to hear how others have coped with loss, and what was and wasn't effective coping behavior. They receive support from many in the group, through their tears and laughter. Members in the group will engage each other. A group member may recognize many personalities that are similar to those in his life where a struggle exists and find tools to confront and work through the feelings associated with feeling intimidated. Feedback is given, solutions offered, maladaptive patterns are recognized and counsel given for proactive change.

Groups form guidelines in conjunction with the therapist's input. Some groups may want clients' commitment of several months in attendance for continuity reasons. If a group member comes to the session under the influence of drugs or alcohol, he is dismissed from the session, and must address this issue in order to return to the group. Too many absences must be addressed and rules about confidentiality should be reviewed periodically.

Groups are effective for a host of therapy issues: eating disorders, depression, panic disorders, shyness, anger and rage issues, sexual abuse trauma, divorce adjustment, and others. My professional associates and I offered several groups. We provided two groups for adult-male sex offenders of children, both had co-therapists of one male and one female. In conjunction with the perpetrator's group, a woman's group whose husbands or boy-friends had sexually abused theirs and other children were facilitated by both a male and a female therapist. A therapy group of adolescent sexually abused girls were facilitated by two female therapists. Additionally, a woman's issue group, having one female therapist, was available. The choice of two therapists, of different gender or same gender, proved to be valuable to the group processes. The reasons for this statement go beyond the scope of this book, and it is only mentioned to elaborate on the many options available through group psychotherapy. Essentially, the therapy orientation was eclectic with the above noted groups. Therapy groups may have the theoretical focus of any of the previously discussed therapy models. The role of the therapist is basically of a facilitator, observing dynamics, commenting when necessary, and encouraging growth in its members. Usually the group members set the session agenda.

If you are interested in participating in a group, you will be best served by calling local provider agencies to see what is available in your community. Asking about the qualifications of the therapist conducting groups is advised. Usually the therapist will evaluate you to determine your suitability or eligibility for a group. Your suitability is generally established by interview with the therapist, rather than through psychological testing.

Family Therapy

The family unit evolved to provide love, support, protection, and security. When all of its parts fit into an integrated whole, all members benefit. There are numerous stressors that can threaten this structure in part or in whole, and when that happens, an appropriate examination of the relationships needs to be done. What are some of the stressors that can have significant impact on the family? They are numerous, and I will list only a few. You will probably be able to add to my list. Death of a family member, especially when it's a child, divorce, remarriage and a blended family, serious physical or mental illness, acute and chronic sibling rivalry, financial reversals, sexual orientation issue of a family member, sexual abuse, and violence within the home, are just some of the dynamics suitable for family psychotherapy. Family therapy allows the family to meet in a setting, under the guidance of a therapist, to reduce the hurt, to reintegrate, and to heal. It allows them the planned time to address individual and family issues that they might not do at home.

Family therapists may employ any of the major therapy orientations discussed, or an eclectic model. You also may want to ask your potential family therapist if she uses a *structured or systems model.* Those, who do use the systems model, will have credentials of special training. Its basic philosophy holds the view that the family acts as an integrated system and the actions of one member creates a ripple response on all members, and usually a counter reaction in its members. Simply put, all members of a family are affected by and react to each member, and the family unity is affected. Goals of family therapy are to reduce stress and anxiety, and help individual family members regain a sense of self and re-engage into the family unit.

Usually one therapist facilitates family group sessions, but on several occasions, and with very complex family dynamics operating in larger families, I have utilized another therapist who was female.

Play Therapy

In the many years of my clinical practice, I've spent hundreds and hundreds of hours in delightful play with children. In our psychotherapy center, one large room was designated as the play therapy room. It was filled with various toys, games, dolls representing family units, play dough, children's books, a play kitchen, blocks, puzzles, specialized game boards, both regular and therapeutic cards, posters, literately a miniature toy store. Many of the toys, games and books were specially designed for play therapy. It had bright colored shelves and cabinets that were built by members of the males in the adult sex offenders groups we conducted. It was their idea to build the shelving and cabinetry as a small part in their restitution to the victimized children. Children from ages of two to early teens found play therapy a means of relating their conflicts, sadness, anxieties, losses, fears, traumas, and family dynamics through symbolic play. Imagine a young child trying to verbally express the lost of a parent, or the fear of the bully that results in his refusal to go to school, or the trauma of abuse, all with verbal expression. Play is a natural form of expression for children. I recall the adolescent boy who was most reticent to talk to me, and his responses to questions were monosyllables, without any eye contact. I had learned from his foster parents his interest in playing chess. So, we played chess, tens of games. He began to talk as he stared at the game board, opening up his bottled-up feeling about his natural mom, who had abandoned him, and a father he never knew. Or the little girl, who takes the doll symbolic of her father and beats it against the floor, or the poorly self-esteemed kid who cheats in the games we play, or the child whose drawings in play therapy are always adults with frowns, and the self drawings of a boy, always represented without arms----these and hundreds of other play therapy experiences reflect the use of play therapy with children.

Children are brought to play therapy for numerous reasons. It may be due to child jealousy or rivalry of a sibling, school failure in spite of ability, coping with Attention Deficient Disorder with or without Hyperactivity, extreme shyness, compulsive eating disorder, anger management, phobias, enuresis (wetting) and encopresis (soiling), adjustment to divorce, the remarriage of a parent, and many of the same issues an adult may experience. Children are not miniature adults, and play therapy is geared to them. Parent involvement is crucial.

Because so many children are unable to put their feelings and thoughts into words, play therapy offers them another modality in expression. There are children who are verbally expressive, articulate about their thoughts and feeling, and can function with traditional "talk therapy." Yet I find that even with these children, occasional sessions in play therapy provide them a delightful break from one-to-one dialog. On occasion, parents and siblings are invited to a play therapy session.

The therapy orientation in play therapy may be psychodynamic, humanistic, behaviorist, or eclectic. With older children, I have used the cognitive-behavioral model and, as issues arise, a psychodynamic model. Play therapy assists in diagnosis, and provides a supportive venue for issues of affective disorders such as depression, and anxiety.

Karen Horney, (1885-1952), a famous psychoanalyst, in her work in child development said, "You don't fool children." The therapist must be trained to work with children, must desire working with children, and "be real and genuine." If these conditions are not sensed by the child, they will not want to relate to you or return to therapy.

Parents and guardians of children need to ask about the credentials of a therapist. You should always meet first with the therapist; provide history, medical information, reports, etc. At the same time, engage your emotional barometer toward the therapist. If you are not comfortable, trust your impression, and find another therapist. When you get to Chapter 6, a more comprehensive review of "children and adolescents in psychotherapy," is presented.

Brief Therapy

I believe the reader should have some knowledge on "Brief Therapy," but I wasn't quite sure where to put this section in the book. So I guess right here will work. Brief therapy is also known as "cost effective," "time sensitive," and "time effective," therapies. Most of the information contained in this section is from Budman and Gurman's (1988) book, *"Theory and Practice of Brief Therapy."* Their book takes a comprehensive look at the on-going development of brief therapy. While the book is primary directed to the professional therapist, I believe anyone interested in receiving counseling, would find this volume easy to read and most informative.

First, how many visits (sessions) constitute brief therapy, 5, 8, less than 20**?** Budman and Gurman cite studies and "found that most patients discontinued treatment well before 20 visits, with the median number in most settings being 5-6 sessions."(Budman & Gurman, pg.5). Other studies report a median number of sessions to be 8, with over 80% discontinuing their treatment prior to the 20th visit. There is some consensus that 20-25 sessions as representing the upper limit of brief therapy. Essentially, brief therapy is defined as under 20 sessions, regardless of the therapy orientations of psychoanalytic, behavioral, cognitive, humanistic or eclectic. The authors also make another important point. There are "planned brief therapy" and "unplanned brief therapy by default." Planned brief therapies are by design, meaning that the client and therapist, both recognizing the diagnosis, decide on the therapy model or method of treatment and agree on the number of sessions to reach the therapy goals. Brief therapy by default simply means that the therapy is briefer when compared to the norm of psychoanalytic psychotherapies. With the advent of insurance managed care programs, that closely monitor the course of treatment, set limits on the number of sessions, and require authorization for further sessions, more and more therapists have moved toward planned brief therapy.

I recognized early in my practice that "more is not necessarily better" relative to a therapy outcome. How much therapy is enough, still remains an elusive question to answer. Yet, when the client and the therapist agree on the issues (problems), decide on treatment direction and goals, set a reasonable number of sessions, and then re-evaluate to see if more sessions are needed, planned brief therapy is workable and effective. Research continues to demonstrate that quality of the relationship between therapist and client is one of the better indicators of therapy's success, and I believed that the therapist/client relationship is fostered by the brief therapy format. It's also my observation that when clients are fully aware of the set number of sessions, they seem to be more motivated, and more likely to do their homework. It is the firm opinion of many mental health providers that *not all psychological disorders* lend themselves to a brief therapy format. When emotional dysfunctions are clearly defined, such as stress related issues, phobias, some anxiety and depressive disorders, grief issues, marital discord, and behavioral problems of children and adolescents, to name a few, brief therapy may be quite effective. Some personality disorders have to be carefully evaluated as to whether brief therapy is the appropriate therapy format.

You may wish to address, with your perspective therapist, the number of sessions anticipated, relative to your emotional ills. Also, sessions do not necessarily have to be scheduled on a one per weekly basis. With a majority of my clients, scheduling initially may be on a once a week basis, for a month or two, but then become more spread out. "Therapy burn-out" can occur if therapy sessions are too frequently scheduled or too intense, and a week or two weeks break may allow the client to "digest" the therapy content covered. It's appropriate to ask these questions. Don't hesitate to ask. Remember she is working for you.

Chapter 5: Important Issues to Understand in Therapy

Psychological Testing:

With children and adults who seek psychotherapy, psychological testing may or may not be indicated or necessary. However, when indicated it can provide not only assistance for diagnosis, but for direction in treatment. Licensed psychologists in specialty areas of clinical and counseling, are trained to perform a variety of psychological tests. Tests to determine cognitive (intelligence) function, perceptual-motor functions, personality disorders, emotional issues, academic/achievement levels, brain injury (performed by neuropsychologists), may all be part of a battery of "tests." School psychologists are often involved in determining learning disorders and attention deficient problems. With children, in public schools, special education departments may evaluate your child for special placements, and even through a long waiting list of students to be evaluated usually exits, parents have a right to initiate and mandate the testing. Licensed psychologists supervise master level diagnosticians.

In medicine, physicians will run various diagnostic tests to confirm or refute a diagnosis. Psychologists also may want clarification through testing to assist in differential diagnosis, and seek direction for treatment. Psychological testing may also benefit other professional entities such as physicians, attorneys, the courts, or schools.

Your attending psychologist will want to explain why psychological testing is indicated, and go over the results with you. If a psychological report on you or your child is to be sent out of the office, it must have your consent. The psychologist should stay within the boundaries of her training in psycho-diagnostics, and if not, refer you to other psychologists with the special training. It is within your rights as a client to ask about training and experience in psychological testing. Psychiatrists often refer their patients to a licensed psychologist for testing.

As noted, not all clients who enter psychotherapy require psychological testing. Through clinical interviewing with clients who clearly manifest a disorder, through collateral reports from physicians, and others, a clear diagnosis may be obtained. Affective disorders (depression, anxiety) and most personality disorders are readily diagnosed by an experienced therapist.

If you, your child or adolescent are recommended for psychological testing that includes a measure of intelligence, you need to be aware of those "tests" that have the highest validity and reliability. There are numerous measures of cognitive/intelligence, but the following are considered the best instruments to measure these functions.

Stanford-Binet Intelligence Scale (children through adulthood)

Wechsler Preschool and Primary Scale of Intelligence (WPPSI) (ages 3 through 8)

Wechsler Intelligence Scale for Children (WISC) (ages 6 through 16)

Wechsler Adult Intelligence Scale (WAIS) (ages 16 through adulthood)

Make sure the evaluator is using the most recent revised form of the above noted instruments. Special Education Departments will mandate the use of the Stanford-Binet or one of the Wechsler Scales to assist in determination of a student placement. So, if you are getting a private evaluation performed by a psychologist, make sure she uses one of these instruments in obtaining a cognitive measure of your child's ability.

Let's just mention another evaluation inventory

that is commonly used by psychologists. It is called the Minnesota Multiphasic Personality Inventory (MMPI). It measures ten major aspects of personality and contains additional supplementary scales. It is a self-report inventory, where the respondent answers a large number (567) of statements as "true" or "false" about themselves. While there are scales that measure, "faking good" or "faking bad" patterns, it relies on people to tell the truth. When used with additional instruments in a battery of tests, the MMPI can be beneficial in diagnosis and treatment.

Mention should be made of a special category of psychologists, involved in testing, called forensic psychologists, which is simply the pairing of the law and psychology. These specialty trained evaluators perform evaluations for competency to stand trial, to determine their ability to assist in their defense, in sanity hearing (insanity is a legal term, not a psychological term), and perhaps in child custody issues. In addition, psychologists who specialize with children and adolescents are trained in diagnostics for a variety of learning disorders. Lastly, neuropsychologists are trained in evaluations of how the brain and its functions are integrated with behavior and emotions. These specially trained psychologists can also assist in the determination of brain damage, working closely with a neurologist, a physician.

There are literally hundreds of psychological tests that can be used by psychologists, depending on the area of interest that she wishes to probe in assisting diagnosis and for direction in treatment. As a client, don't be timid to ask why you are being tested, and the training of the psychologist.

Understanding Your Diagnosis

You will be given a diagnosis, by your psychiatrist, psychologist, social worker, or other licensed mental health practitioners, including physicians, nurses, occupational and rehabilitation therapists, both in outpatient and inpatient facilities. The language and words used in the descriptive definitions of the diagnoses are applicable to all the different psychological orientations described in this book. If you are filing an insurance claim for your treatment, the insurance provider will require a diagnosis from the mental health provider. All diagnoses are uniformly obtained from the *Diagnostic and Statistical Manual of Mental Disorders (DSM)*. The most recent revised edition, at the time of this writing, is entitled, DSM-*IV-TR (text revised) (4th Edition, c2000).* It is a collaborative effort of the American Psychiatric Association and other task forces designed to be consistent, accurate, and communicative in this massive attempt to design a diagnostic format. It is revised when research and empirical evidence justifies revision, or when greater clarity is needed. Copies of DSM-IV-TR can be found (and purchased) at major retail bookstores, and in libraries as referenced books.

Let's explain how the diagnostic scheme is done. A multi-axial system was designed, unitizing five (5) axes. Each axis represents one specific information-communication of the diagnosis, information on medical condition, social and environmental stressors, and overall level of current functioning. Let's put this in a list form for better clarity:

Axis I Clinical Disorders

Axis II Personality Disorders

(mental retardation conditions are classified as Axis II)

Axis III General Medical Conditions

Axis IV Psychosocial and Environmental Problems

Axis V Global Assessment of Functioning (GAF)

Still with me? Let's suppose you have had some sessions with your therapist, and maybe some psychological testing was done, and you ask your therapist if she has determined a diagnosis. She says "yes." You have a pretty good ideal that it has to be in the depression area, but you ask, "Well, what is it, Doc?" She says, "Let me explain your full diagnosis," and shows you a page in your file that has a listing of Axis I through Axis V. You listen to her explanation.

"Bill, your clinical condition on (Axis I) is Dysthymic Disorder, which simply means a chronic depressed mood, that you reported for at least the last four years. You have reported feeling "down", with low energy levels, difficulty sleeping, lost of appetite, a loss of interest in activities that usually bring you enjoyment, and some self-esteem issues. You have also reported concentration problems at work, and your wife complains of your lack of interest in sexual intimacy. The MMPI also indicated an elevated "depression scale." You remember, we went over the results of the MMPI, and one of the scales that measured bodily complaints, was elevated. Since the depression did not manifest itself until you were in your forty's, it's called "late-onset" dysthymic disorder. You are not experiencing a "major depression." Your Axis I diagnosis is "Dysthymic Disorder, Late Onset."

"On Axis II, which has to do with Personality Disorders, you are not afforded a diagnosis, as there is no evidence of a personality dysfunction. So your Axis II results in "no diagnosis."

"On Axis III, which deals with any medical conditions associated to your mild-to-moderate, chronic depression, I've listed insomnia. The work-up by your physician did not report any medical problems. Your Axis III is "insomnia."

"Axis IV indicates if there are any environmental stressors creating a social or psychological impact in your life, as related to your Axis I diagnosis. You have some concerns with marital dissatisfaction, and in my interview with your wife, she shares the same concerns. Your work production, by your report, has fallen and you worry about your job security. Thus, "marital stress and fear of job loss" are noted.

"Lastly, Axis V. This has to do with my judgment of how well you are functioning with the diagnosis of depression, on Axis I, and those other factors impinging upon you *at this time*. It ranges from 1 to 100. The lower the score, the poorer you are viewed in general functioning. This score may be altered at the time that therapy is completed, but at this time, your GAF is 45. This is simply my impression. Do you have any questions?"

Axis I and Axis II have coded numbers. For the example above:

Axis I: 300.40 (Dysthymic Disorder)
Axis II: V71.09 (no diagnosis)
Axis III: Insomnia
Axis IV: Marital Stress/Fear of Job Loss
Axis V: 45

Do you have a right to know and discuss your diagnosis? A simple answer is *YES!*

We will discuss confidentially issues in psychotherapy in a later part of this book, and will discuss the issue of "diagnosis confidentially" as part of this section.

Ready for another joke or two?

A guy goes to see a psychologist. He says, "It seems I can't make any friends. Can you help me, you fat slob?"

Why is psychoanalysis a lot quicker for a man than for a woman?
Because when it's time to go back to childhood, a man is already there.

Understanding Your Rights to Confidentiality, Privacy, and Privilege.

Every State Board of Examiners in Psychology has statues and laws that govern the confidentiality of the client in psychotherapy. But, it is the psychotherapist who represents the first line in protection of clients' rights, and she should be fully cognizant of the statues and laws. While each state may have minor differences in their statues, the primary goals are the same, that is, the therapist takes reasonable precautions to protect confidential information of their clients. Please recall that I practiced in Louisiana, and thus my frame of reference is with its board of examiners, and Louisiana laws and statues. Your therapist will be familiar with your state's statues.

Most clients have a vague knowledge of confidentiality when they enter psychotherapy, in that; the therapist cannot disclose information shared by the client. Most clients simply assume "that's how it works." They (the clients) can tell "whomever" what was said in a therapy session, but the therapist does not have that right. Seldom do clients ask about confidentiality. On the information sheets that I give to clients are statements that address their rights of confidentiality, but the complexity of this issue cannot be fully dissimulated in this format.

To create a psychologically safe place for the client to share their most intimate thoughts, feelings, secrets, and regrettable behaviors of the past, they must sense that the client-therapist association is sacrosanct. Otherwise, they will be reluctant to disclose fully, which may impede the therapy process. Let's go over some of the issues of confidentiality, privacy, and privilege. At this point, I am addressing *adult* clients in treatment. Later there will be some discussion of minor children and the sticky issue with adolescents.

You may notice that the therapist keeps a file or chart. The chart will have dates of your sessions, notes on each session, results of any psychological testing, medical reports that were sent by your physician (with your consent), payment records, your diagnosis and clinical statements about your treatment. The therapist creates the file, but you have a right to know what is in the file. In essence, it is yours. Information, in part or in total, from your file cannot be divulged or sent from the office without your signed consent (release of information form). If your records are subpoenaed by a court, you will be asked to sign a release form, consenting only to the person, or agency requesting your records. If you refuse, a court (judge) may order the therapist to release the file or be in contempt of a court order. Some subpoenas may ask for a summary report of the file, or the file in its entirety (Subpoena Duces Tecum) which is usually the case, and in addition, a possible mandate to testify in court. A client needs to recognize that a therapist can and will protect your records, but if the records are subpoenaed Duces Tecum, they must be turned over to the court.

In addition, there are other situations that you need to be aware of that expose your privacy of treatment. If you file insurance, and sign an authorization for your psychotherapist to give information to your insurance carrier, others will be privy to your diagnosis; numbers of sessions attended, and even a statement of a prognosis. Managed-care insurance companies often require very specific information on a consumer, perhaps more than clients with private insurance. Once this information is in the possession of the insurance company, there is no control on who views it.

Your therapist will act by statues and laws that protect your confidentiality and privacy. However, there are exceptions which can allow the therapist, or require the therapist to release confidentiality information. *These exceptions are mandated by law.* Let's review the exceptions.

1. State law requires the therapist to report the abuse and neglect of a child, the elderly or any disabled person when there is reasonable evidence and belief that it occurred.

2. The psychotherapist must act to protect the client if there is reasonable evidence of suicide, and if there is a direct threat to harm other persons, by the client. Confidentiality will be breached by the therapist who will need to inform others of the intentions of the client. This is called the "duty to warn" statue.

There have been several occasions, relative to exception #1, where I was mandated to report sexual, emotional, physical abuse, or neglect of a child or adolescent by my client. If the abuser of the child is "within the home," Child Protection Services is notified and the alleged abuse is investigated. If the abuser of the child is "not within the home," police authorities are notified and they investigate the allegation.

Relative to exception #2, in my many years of practice, there were only two cases where a "duty to warn" was necessary. One case involved a clinically depressed adolescent who articulated suicidal statements, noting the method he planned to use and his availability of guns within his home. He was told I would inform his parents and recommend inpatient treatment for his protection.

This was accomplished and I continued to follow him while in the hospital and upon his discharge.

The other experience involved a client with an adjustment disorder of depression and anxiety, who was seriously physically injured on a job. He frequently expressed anger at his current attorney (he fired several others) for dragging out his case, not returning calls, etc. He made a direct threat to harm his attorney, carried a registered weapon in his car, and presented a reasonable threat to the attorney. He was told of my mandate to inform his attorney of his intent to harm him, and I did so immediately. The client was present in my office when I informed the attorney. A release of information to his attorney was already in my file, but under this circumstance, unnecessary.

Mental health providers often consult on some of their cases with other psychotherapists. In my opinion, this is a benefit of a group practice as I mentioned early in this book. Several knowledgeable opinions are better than one. In my group practice, it was a standard procedure for the therapists to consult with each other on their cases, which I think benefited the clients. While content of the case may be discussed, no identifying information is disclosed. The client's confidentiality and privacy are protected.

Consent must be obtained from the client to record, audio or video, a therapy session or a testing session or any contact with a client. Any use of the client's file for research can only be used with signed consent and the assurance of all identifying information is not included.

Next, let's get into the murky issues of *confidentiality of children and adolescents* when they are the clients. Things can get complicated. Depending on the respective state law, who holds privilege may vary. Is it the child/adolescent or the legal parent(s)? Generally, it is the parents or legal guardian who holds privilege. There are factors of custody proceedings that further complicate this issue. When a therapist has a need to inform parents on the disposition of therapy, good reasoning is necessary on the part of the therapist. Not all information needs to be shared. I believe this is certainly true with adolescents, whose trust in the therapist is even more vital. If there is not a "hostile or adversarial" issue between parents (custody battle, divorce), protection of child privacy and privilege can be negotiated. In most states, the file record of a child should not be destroyed until he reaches the "age of majority." You should ask your therapist about your state laws or statues by the governing Board of Examiners, relative to confidentiality issues with children and teens.

Confidentiality in Group Psychotherapy

Once a group is formed, one of the immediate issues the therapist(s) and group members need to address is confidentiality. It is important for the group members to understand, and appreciate that "what is discussed in the group, stays in the group." The members of the group however cannot be assured that some or all members would not reveal private matters to others outside the group. If content is revealed to outside sources, all identifying information of a group member must be excluded. Each time a new member joins the group, the issue of confidentiality is repeated. As stated earlier, this should be addressed periodically in the ongoing group. The same issue needs to be addressed in couples and family therapies. On occasion, an individual session is required with one member, then that session must remain private from the couple or family therapies. If a request for information on the couple or family therapies is made, all members must consent.

I have not exhausted all the issues involved with this topic. At one level, it is simple. The therapist guards the confidentiality for the client, informs the clients of the exceptions, and maintains an honest relationship in the client-therapist alliance. At another level, the issues in confidentiality can become complicated, and when this occurs, the client should consult the therapist for clarity and the therapist should consult his peers and governing boards, statues, and laws for direction and guidance.

Another joke?

Psychiatrist to his nurse: "Just say we are busy. Don't keep saying, "It's a mad house in here."

Psychotherapy Fees and Insurance, Managed Care and Brief Therapy

The cost of psychotherapy varies significantly. Usually, but not a rule, psychiatrists' fees may be higher than psychologists, psychologists higher than social workers, and social workers higher than counselors with a variety of professional labels. Fees will vary in different regions of the country. A client should inquire as to the specific fees charged per session and if there is a higher fee for the in-take (first) session. Will the therapist wait for payment from the insurance company, or be expected to be paid "up front" per session? Will you have to pay for missed appointments and under what circumstances? Will the therapist's office file the insurance forms? Also, does the therapist accept only what the insurance company will pay per session? What about them paying your fees if therapy extends beyond the total number of sessions allowed? Enter the managed care provider programs. In the early 1980's managed care, such as HMO's, has become a force in all health providers' practice, and psychotherapy was no exception. Brief therapy formats were necessary to accommodate the fixed number of sessions allowed, relative to diagnosis or not. This is decided by managed care "case reviewers." Also, the psychotherapist must accept the fee per session amount established by the managed care provider. Your managed care company will provide you with a list of the therapist in and around your community who made application and are approved by the company. This arrangement may preclude you from seeing a therapist based on your personal choice or through others' recommendations. If you wish to see a therapist not listed as a provider on your plan, you have to pay all costs. If your therapist believes you need more than, say the twenty sessions approved by managed care, and you agree to continue, you are responsible for the additional sessions. As a consequence of the managed care movement, many therapists have opted for orientations in psychotherapy that lend themselves to brief therapy.

I have attended workshops when I was in practice, directed at the influence of managed care on mental health providers. I witnessed many mental health providers vent much frustration and angst toward managed care companies. I held several listings as a managed care provider, and I had very mixed opinions of its influence on me as a psychotherapist. I also witnessed the frustration of the client who felt limited to the regimentation of managed care plans. My frustration was greatest on those cases when clients had a diagnosis of personality disorders, which often required more intensive and longer duration in therapy. The frustration was compounded in working with a case manager reviewer who did not have the understanding or appreciation of these and other more complex diagnoses. I spend many hours on the phone, in the filing of reports, and in requesting additional sessions for my clients. I reached a point where I resigned as a provider to these managed care companies. Fortunately, my practice had a viable referral base, which allowed me to make that decision. On the positive side, managed care did provide greater accountability in providing psychological care to its customers, by requiring effective therapy methods. It did move psychotherapy to briefer forms of therapy, and perhaps, a more cost-effective model in treatment. There are two sides to the issue of managed care, and I hope the many issues will be resolved, not to the detriment of the client.

Take a break. A managed care joke seems to be appropriate at this point.

A psychologist in a bar leans over to the guy next to him and says, "Wanna hear a managed care joke?"
The guy next to him replies," Well before you tell that joke, you should know something. I'm 6' tall, and weigh 200 lbs., and I'm a managed care lawyer. The guy sitting next to me is 6' 2" tall, weighs 225, and he's a managed care supervisor. The fellow next to him is 6' 5' tall, and weighs 250, and he's one of our second level reviewers. Now, you still want to tell that joke?"
The psychologist says, "Nah. I don't want to have to explain it three times."

Professional Ethics in Psychotherapy

My intent in this section is not to go over the numerous established rules of ethics in the client/therapist relationship. There are indeed many, some with clear parameters, others are less clear, and can lead to confusion and misunderstanding by both clients and therapists. However, with that said, the therapist has the responsibility to know the professional ethics as set forth by his governing board and the American Psychological Association (APA).

Clients seek therapy and, in that effort, they are placing themselves in the trust of therapists and the training and skills they possess. There is client vulnerability, coupled with the confusion of thoughts, feelings, and dysfunctional behaviors. Their focus is to resolve the issues through treatment. The therapist should not add to these issues with unethical behaviors. Your therapist is afforded authority, power, and trust and she should never violate these important conditions. Your therapist may shake your hand, but cannot be your sex partner; your therapist can help you evaluate your work stressors but cannot be your business partner; your therapist cannot be your landlord, or your relative; your therapist cannot swap (barter) services with you in exchange for her professional therapy fees; your therapist cannot withhold your records that are requested/needed by others, because therapy fees have not been paid; your therapist cannot accept expensive gifts from you, and there are many other issues the therapist should be aware of in order to safeguard your trust in her. If you feel uncomfortable in any situation with your therapist's behavior or intent, it should be addressed with the therapist. In Louisiana, licensed psychologists must display in a prominent place, usually the waiting room, a plaque offering the address of the Louisiana Board of Examiners in Psychology. This allows a client to register a written complaint if he chooses. I'm sure other states require similar arrangements.

The important issue of ethics is valid in all professional services, whether it is with your physician, attorney, or clergy. Boundaries are established by governing agencies, and it is important that the professionals offering services keep abreast of the rules and regulations. The client's responsibility is to work diligently toward the resolution of their issues, without their rights being violated by the therapist.

Chapter 6: Children and Adolescents in Psychotherapy

In the many years of my clinical practice, I treated hundreds of children and adolescents with psychological disorders. On rare occasions, I saw children in psychotherapy who had informed their parents or guardians that they, "wanted to talk to somebody," implying a psychotherapist. They were usually precocious kids, or perhaps those who watched too much television. Rarer were the teens that approached their caretakers and requested "to see a shrink." However, by far, children and adolescents are brought to see a therapist by their parents, some willingly, most not so willingly.

Then, there were those children, teens and parents who believed that seeing a therapist was a measure of status obtainment. Having said that, most parents were very sincere in their concerns and most had tried various means to resolve the troubling issues themselves, or within their family unit. Most had consulted their friends, teachers, school counselors, and physicians before seeking a psychotherapist. A majority of the parents had read self-help books, surf the internet, attended community workshops, all in order to learn more about their children's symptoms, causes and treatments, relative to their disturbing observations. Generally, parents were significantly motivated to get help for their children, with greater zeal, perhaps, than for concerns of themselves. The majority were willing to attend parenting classes, or be involved in couples or family therapies. Almost all of the parents wanted assurance that their parenting was appropriate, and if not, willing to listen and try alternative approaches. Some had concerns about genetic and hereditary influences impacting their children. And a much smaller percentage of parents simply wanted the therapist to "fix the problem," so they could go about their busy lives, too busy to get involved with family, couples-therapy, or parenting classes. All parents soon realized that their child's psychotherapy required a full commitment by them.

What are some of the reasons children and teens are brought to the psychotherapist's office? The clinical issues are not so different from the adult client. Children and adolescents experience depression, anxiety disorders, adjustment problems to divorce, loss of a love one, sleep disorders, traumatic experiences such as victimization, phobias, drug and alcohol abuse, serious emotional disorders, to name a few. *Special age-related dysfunctions* may be separation anxiety, enuresis and encopresis (soiling oneself), developmental delays, autism, oppositional-defiant, conduct disorder, Tourette's, and selective mutism, again, to name a few.

When working with the child or adolescent client, it is equally important for the therapist and the parents to make sure that a comprehensive physical/medical examination is performed to rule out any medical cause contributing to the suspected psychological disorder. For example, with the diagnosis of enuresis, the need to rule out untreated diabetes or urinary tract infection is important to note. Mental health providers must be willing to consult with medical specialists, establish a compatible, not a competitive relationship, all in the best interest of the child. Psychologists, social workers and other mental health professionals who possess a rigid, negative bias toward any medication use or other medical procedure, are to be suspect as an appropriate therapist for your child or teen. The same can be said of psychiatrists and other medical specialists who hold the belief that psychotherapy ("talking therapies") has minimal or no value in the dysfunctions of children. Regardless of the specific professional discipline that may have initially screened for possible mental, emotional, physical, or behavioral problems, working with children involves a multi-discipline approach. For example, on many cases with a child in psychotherapy, I may have consulted with the youngster's teacher(s), school counselor, speech and language therapist, and a physician.

Let's not forget the most important "professional" in the mix, the parents of the child or adolescent. It is the parents who understand their child in the most comprehensive and thorough manners. I always told parents, "I won't pretend to know your children as well as you do. So, it's very important that you discuss with me your full knowledge of your child without reservation, in both your positive and negative evaluations. You, as caretakers of your child are the experts on his growth and development, and you can provide me with keen insights that I can't get from psychological, school or medical reports. Be candid with your thoughts and feelings about your child. I will value, respect and trust your perceptions." With that said, let's move onto some important topics that hopefully will prepare you in obtaining the right therapy and therapist for your child and teen.

How will you know if your child or adolescent needs psychotherapy?

Independent of various degrees of denial, most parents know something is amiss with their kids. They are not functioning properly. Something is wrong. You sense a change in behavior, attitude, or in the emotions expressed in your youngsters. You wait to see if "things will get back to normal, or maybe they will out-grow it." It doesn't, so you discuss your concerns with your spouse. There may be agreement or disagreement in the observations you both have made. You talk to your child. You get little information. You continue to monitor your concerns. Things seem to get worse. You read articles; consult your child's pediatrician, family and friends. You start trusting yourself. Something is wrong. Sometimes what is wrong may be very obvious, such as the consequence of an environmental event, moving to a new city, loss through death of a family member, a new school, break-up of a friendship, and countless number of events that can impact upon your child. Sometimes, there appears to be no direct cause-effect explanation. Yet, your child's grade performance drops, he is sullen or angry, eating and sleeping patterns change and when your child or teen are addressed by family members, there is non-responsive silence. Attention needs to be focused on these issues and parents need to consult with a physician and/or child psychologist. You will know when and if your child needs therapy. Trust your parental intuition.

Child or teen symptoms of emotional distress that require immediate response by parents.

(The symptoms listed below mainly come from Dr. T. E. Wilens' book, "Straight Talk about Psychiatric Medications for Kids," listed in the reference chapter.)

- Verbal threats and actions of harming themselves (suicidal ideation and gestures).
- Severe emotional tantrums and anger/rage fueled attacks upon others and upon property.
- Pronounced isolation and withdrawal from family and friends.
- Threats to harm someone because of perceived (real or imagined) threats upon themselves.
- Rapid and marked weight loss without medical cause, which may indicate an eating disorder.
- Hearing or seeing things that are not present (auditory or visual hallucinations).
- Evidence of drug or alcohol abuse.
- Prolonged absence from home without parent permission or knowledge, and marked truancy from school.
- Minimal or no evidence of remorse

when they have emotionally or physically aggressed upon others.

The above examples of pathology (illness) should be taken as definitive "cries for help," and there should be *no negotiation* with the child or adolescent if there is reluctance on their part to receive professional help. The above symptoms generally reflect serious emotional, behavioral and thought disorders. Now let's move onto the next step in getting mental health assistance for your children.

How do you get children and particularly teens to the psychotherapist and cooperate with the therapy process?

It has been my experience that children and adolescents who experience depression, phobias, anxiety disorders, especially accompanied by panic attacks, are more likely to agree to counseling, than those who exhibit conduct disorders, oppositional-defiant behavior, extreme sibling rivalry, learning disorders, and attention deficient disorder, with or without hyperactivity. Why? In the former, they feel bad and want help to remedy the pain. In the latter, they don't perceive a problem, and it's easy to blame events outside of themselves as responsible. Thus in the former, the manifestation of distress is internalized, and in the latter, the distress is externalized. Regardless, some strategy for assistance is needed.

How do you approach a child about agreeing to psychotherapy? First step, is to tell the child, using only "I statements," that you are concerned for them. Here is an example. "Billy, I'm worried about how sad you seem lately. This makes me feel helpless, and I don't like feeling that way. I don't know how to help. Dad and I are concerned that you are not happy, and we don't understand why, and maybe you don't either. Remember we went to see your medical doctor and he examined you to see if you were O.K.? He said you were physically all right. Dad and I have scheduled an appointment with a different kind of doctor. She talks with kids your age to help them work through their problems----no, she doesn't give shots, just talk, and maybe play games with you to get to know you. Perhaps you can talk to her. Mom and Dad will meet with her first, just to tell her our concerns, and to see if we like her. If we like her and believe she might be able to help, would you see her? Think about it, O.K.? She may be able to help us to help you." I know this may sound a little too Pollyanna, but you get the point. Hopefully the child will get several messages from you. *You* are concerned, *you* have taken steps to help, *you* don't blame *him,* and as a parent, *you* are willing to assist him.

With adolescents, it is perhaps more difficult for parents to convince them to see a therapist. While some of the same ploys that I just described are still valid, trust in adults and authority figures loom greater for the teen. Most teens will have concerns about confidentiality. Will the therapist tell all to my parents? Will the therapist align herself with my parents? Will they put me in a hospital? Do they think I'm crazy? These are reasonable concerns from the perspective of an adolescent. It is important for the parents (and the therapist) to answer these and other questions he might have. Perhaps the best way to approach the teen is for the parents to have their initial consultation with the therapist *before* they approach their child. If asked, the therapist will suggest to the parents some approaches to use in preparing their teen for psychotherapy.

I don't believe in bribing children or adolescents into seeing a therapist. "I'll buy you the video game you've been wanting if you just go see Dr. Therapist." But saying, "I want you to go for five sessions (pick your number) and if you think you are not being helped or you don't like the therapist, you don't have to continue," is appropriate. Finding the right therapist for your teen may require visiting more than one therapist. If the teen is attending the sessions, working at his issues, and demonstrates a positive attitude to the whole process, then giving him that video game at this point, is not a bribe but a positive reinforcement. Remember, therapy is non-negotiable if your child or teen are exhibiting any of the serious distress symptoms previously listed on page 89. Also be aware that teens are capable of sabotaging the therapy process. Usually, it takes the form of passive-aggressive behavior such as," I forgot about the appointment today," or "I didn't feel like talking in today's session, so I just stared at the therapist." There may be direct defiance, "you can't make me go back, and I'm not going," or, 'she (the therapist) is crazy, she's the one who needs help." But don't despair; therapists are trained to deal with these issues of the adolescent. Most children and teens find therapy a place to vent, solve their problems, and enjoy the relationship with the therapist. They are usually surprised to find a professionally trained adult, who will not lecture, criticize, will offer unconditional acceptance, and willingness to help them untangle their sadness, fears, and relationship conflicts. A special alliance develops as it does with adult clients. I've had many adolescents say to me during a session, "You're cool, Doc. You listen."

Characteristics you want to see in your child's psychotherapist.

Not all mental health providers are trained to work with children or adolescents. Not all providers want to work with these age groups. Working with children and teens requires an abundance of the therapist's patience in relating to them at their level. The therapist should possess an ability to frame their language so the child will have an opportunity to understand and to respond. Therapists of children must be able to tolerate hours of interactive or parallel play in the play-therapy room, and not be bored, but intrigued with the process of child play. The therapist must be willing to let the child set the pace of therapy, and perhaps the most significant trait, is the genuine enjoyment of relating to children. Obviously, the therapist must have a comprehensive knowledge of childhood-adolescent growth and development, so the parameters of healthy and dysfunctional patterns are recognized.

I respected those highly skilled psychologists who choose not to work with children and teens, because they recognized they didn't have the temperaments to be effective with these age groups. I know from my experience in working with children, that they often challenged the highest levels of my therapeutic skills, while providing me the highest level of "job satisfaction."

Let's do some "bullets" and list the characteristics (not in any order of importance) that I believe a psychotherapist ought to possess when the client is a child or adolescent.

- An unending reserve of patience.
- An ability to relate with verbal skills at the level of the young person.
- A genuine appreciation and acceptance of the child's current stage of development.
- Ability to tolerate hyperactivity of the child or teen.

- Willingness to allow the child to direct the pace in activities and in conversation.
- A climate in therapy for the child to sense permission to emote (express feelings) and act freely.
- Ability of the therapist to demonstrate an unconditional acceptance of the child's feelings and behaviors. However, this must be clearly established within the boundaries of societal and other relationship expectations.
- Promotion of the concept that the child can solve his own problems, and thus develop problem solving skills that will serve him well into the future.
- With the adolescent client, ability to tolerate passive-aggressive behaviors, such as responding to questions with "I don't know" (the infamous "IDK" response). "Forgetting" to do what he agreed to do (therapy homework), or coming to the session late because he wasn't available at home so a parent could drive him to the therapy session are other examples of this behavior.

- Ability to be patient in *earning the trust* of the teen client.

There are other qualities the therapist should possess but this gives you some insight that the child/teen therapist by training and experience must be unique. Parents need to evaluate the therapist on the noted qualities.

What should parents expect in the initial-parent interview with their child's therapist?

Most, if not all, mental health providers will want to meet and interview the parents or legal guardians of the child or teen before they schedule their children. The reasons are obvious as the child cannot provide developmental history and other crucial information. Most parents have a vague idea as to what the therapist will want in information, principally, what is the parent's view of the child's problem(s). This contact provides the parents an opportunity to gauge their impressions of the therapist. I suggest to parents not to bring the child with them to the parent session, as he may be in the waiting room for an hour or more. This can be scary for the child, and boring for the adolescent. I don't want the child to start off their therapy experience feeling marooned in the waiting room with strangers. Additionally, the time-break between seeing the parents and the child, can be used by the parents to evaluate their impressions of the therapist.

In this section, I will advise the parents on what generally will be asked, and to have the information ready prior to meeting with the therapist. In addition, I want to suggest to the parent questions they may wish to ask the therapist.

While greeting you in the waiting room, the office manager will give you some forms to complete which will ask the usual identifying information, and may contain a space for you to write out your reasons for seeking services for your child. The therapist will review your responses and then call you into her office. I usually reserved at least seventy-five minutes for the intake session with the parents. There is much to establish and learn before the child is seen by the therapist.

What the therapist will most likely want to learn from you.

- How long have you been married, and level of marital satisfaction? If not married, the current status of the relationship?
- Other children, ages, and any concerns with these children.
- Previous marriage(s) and reasons for exiting the marriage. Half or step-sibling in the current family system? Any chronic sibling rivalry issue? Any previous counseling of the current household members?
- Current medications of parents? Psychiatric history of each parents, their biological

parents and their siblings? Any drug or alcohol abuse in the family? Any criminal records of either parent?

- The name of your child's pediatrician and results of the most recent medical work-up. Any medications presently prescribed for the child client? Information on your child's developmental milestones, such as age of walking and talking, may be asked, along with any childhood illnesses that was unusual, and any surgeries? Has the child experienced a loss of consciousness, perhaps from a blow to his head, or sustained high body temperature?
- Your child's school performance, recent and past. Any identified learning disabilities?
- "Tell me your concerns for your child. Why do you think he needs to see a psychotherapist?"

Relative to the last item, I would suggest you spend some time rehearsing, yes, rehearsing your response as to the concerns for your child/teen. Maybe you can write out your thoughts. Please feel free to bring your notes with you to this first session, and refer to them if needed. You want to make sure you cover all of your concerns and observations of your child. The therapist will value your effort. Remember what I wrote in this book. *You are the expert on your child. You know him better than anyone else.* Don't be timid to offer your hypothesis as to what is wrong and maybe even on the etiology (cause) of your child's disorder. How does the following sound to you?

"Doctor, my husband and I are very worried about Billy. Over the last six-month he has become sullen and withdrawn. I'm not sure I would call him depressed, but he seems to worry about a lot of things a ten-year shouldn't be worrying about. Like, in the morning he checks and rechecks his book sack to see if he has all his homework in it. At night he wants to check the doors to see if they are locked, and wants to know if I didn't forget to turn off the stove. I have to keep reassuring him about a lot of things. My husband gets irritated with him, and I have to admit, I lose my temper with him. His brothers call him a "little girl." Each night he lays out his school clothes, all neat, and he gets upset if I change things around in his room. He was never like this before. He made messes like any other kid, but now he has turned into some kind of worry-wart, neat freak. His teachers tell us he has a hard time completing his assignments in school because he has to go over and over his papers before he turns them in. As a result, his grades have fallen. I have an uncle who does weird stuff like wearing the same clothes on certain days of the week, and eating his food in a ritualistic fashion. He told me he was diagnosed obsessive-compulsive by his doctor. Think Billy inherited the same thing? I can't think of anything that would have set-off these behaviors of Billy. Nothing really has changed at home in the last six-months. The only thing he has done outside of the home is to attend a Boy Scout camp this past summer. That was about seven months ago. We are worried, Doctor. He also seems to be getting worse. That's why we scheduled this appointment."

The above is a starting point. Based upon what you shared with the therapist, more questions will follow. It is important to be candid and forthcoming in your responses in the interview session. Next let's look at what you should consider asking the psychotherapist.

What to ask the child's therapist.

- How often will you see my child?
- What therapy approach will you use? Will the approach be used in a play therapy format? Do you have a separate play therapy area? If so, can we see it?
- Can you tell us a little about the therapy approach you will use, and maybe provide a reference for us to read? (The reader is reminded that the psychotherapy orientations were discussed in Chapter 3, and Play Therapy, as a format was provided in Chapter 4.)
- Will you meet with the parents from time-to-time?
- Will you tell us soon what you think is happening with our child, perhaps a diagnosis?

- Will you do any psychological testing with our child? If so, what is the fee?
- Will you make a contact with his homeroom teacher at school?
- Will you consult with his pediatrician?
- We will have to sign a release of information form before you talk to anyone or send reports, correct?
- Have you worked with kids who demonstrated similar problems?
- Will your office file insurance for us?

I'm sure you will think of more questions to ask as the therapy progresses. Don't rely on memory, write them down. *If you felt comfortable after meeting the therapist, great. If not, consider obtaining another referral.* Only entrust a therapist with your child that you have confidence and a belief in her abilities.

Points to remember. The child's therapist has a mandate to dissolve confidentiality if there is a perceived danger to the child, or others, or if there is reasonable evidence of some form of victimization upon your child. Otherwise, your child's therapist will use her discretion as to what information she will divulge to the parents. This is even more of a critical issue when the client is an adolescent. Most teens will judge any collaboration by the therapist with the parents as threatening to his confidentiality privilege. The therapist must balance the parents' need to know while assuring the teen his rights are being protected. This is a delicate tight-rope for the therapist to walk. The parents should respect and trust the therapist's judgment on this issue.

Comments on psychiatric medication and your children.

In Dr. Timothy E. Wilens' book, *Straight Talk About Psychiatry Medications for Kids,* he notes that an estimated 11%-to-22% of American kids or an estimated 7.5-to-14 million suffer from psychiatric disorders.(2004, pg.1) Dr Wilens is a psychiatrist who specializes in children and adolescents. He has written a most informative book to assist parents in their difficult decision (to consent) in the use of psychoactive drugs for their kid's thinking, behavioral or emotional disorders. Dr. Wilens writes a step-by-step process in decision making for parents. He explains all terms. He educates the reader in a manner that is clear, concise, and most valuable for those parents or guardians who are faced with this difficult decision. His book is referenced in Chapter 9.

Since I'm not a medical doctor or a psychiatrist, I'll "speak" only from my experience as a psychologist. There were numerous occasions, while providing psychotherapy and/or upon extensive psychological testing with a child or adolescent, when I believed psychiatric medication might be indicated. I met with the parents, and if the teen was the primary client, he was included in the consult session. With the information gained in counseling sessions, and from results of testing, I reviewed the file material, and recommended an evaluation by a medical specialist. The purposes of which is to further explore if a medical (organic) reason(s) precipitated the manifested disorder, and to evaluate the child for psychiatric or other medication. At his point, I provided several names of medical specialists, with whom I had worked within the past years. This recommendation frequently produced much anxiety for parents. The angst was expected and appropriate. In a current climate where taking a pill to cure our ills is common and accepted ("better living through chemistry"), when children are involved, *careful evaluation must be accomplished before psychiatric medications are implemented in the treatment process.* The parents, in consultation with medical specialists, need to arrive at a measured, thoughtful, and medically based decision. It must be a case-by-case decision, evaluating the specific issues of this child, this teen, not a blanket mentality of, "the child is Attention Deficient Disordered, put him on medication."

It is the responsibility of the non-medical, mental health provider to assist parents in the appropriate steps for further evaluation by a medical specialist, whether it is a pediatrician, a pediatric neurologist, or a psychiatrist. Medication evaluation does not automatically imply a psychiatrist. The mental health provider should not just recommend a medical specialist, and consider her job done. It is her responsibility to continue to consult with the specialist, until the issues are resolved or she is dismissed from further case management by the parents. Psychotherapy along with pharmacotherapy is occasionally indicated and needs to be a unified decision by the psychotherapist, medical specialist, and parents.

Lastly, I have seen children and teens who have received significant benefit with medical specialists prescribing psychoactive medications. Others experienced marginal or no benefit. Again, a case by case evaluation and treatment regiment needs to be accomplished. Parents' hopes, fears and specific questions of children on medications, should be addressed by the medical specialist, not the non-medical, mental health provider. However, the characteristics previously listed as necessary for the mental health provider who work with children and teens, also apply to medical specialists.

Allow me to close out Chapter 6 with a personal editorial observation of children and teens in psychotherapy. I've noted that there are sincere, caring parents who rush to the psychotherapist's office at the first signs of their children's distress. The current Zeitgeist (the spirit of the times) appears to be that if a child's self-esteem or self-concept levels are threatened, "bruised", or diminished by internal or external stressors, they are quickly brought to a psychological or medical specialist. Certainly, preventative psychology is to be commended, but we also need to afford children and teens an opportunity to cope, restore homeostasis (balance), and develop problem solving skills. If we rush them to outside sources (therapists) that will assist them to resolve stresses, a degree of independent problem solving is lost. A dependency may even be nurtured. An opportunity to gain confidence in themselves is missed.

Children and adolescents are for the most part, resilient. They are not so psychologically fragile, that we as caretakers of our youth, must over-protect them, and over-nurture them at the slightest sign of distress. They coped with 9-11-2001, hurricanes, the bully at school, the divorce of parents, failing grades, and a large host of events in the complexity of their existence. Most children and teens cope well. Others struggle but eventually achieve resolution on their own. Some don't cope well, and need the assistance of loving, supportive parents. An even smaller number of children may require outside-of-the-family professional help. The point is to not underestimate children's natural resilience to stressors. Zealous parents who over react to the natural sadness, disappointments, anger or acting-out of their children, need to pause, talk to your kid, and wait. Wait to see if the child/teen will work it out on their own. As stated earlier in this chapter, if a child demonstrates the *extreme symptoms* noted, then "rush to therapy."

I have seen a number of children in psychotherapy, who after a session or two, I viewed the issues presented by parents, as over reactive. Brief counseling with the parents was sufficient to assist the child to cope without the professional help of a therapist. Loving and caring for your child is adequate and psychologically sound. Over loving and over caring may foster inability of the child to develop autonomy and hinder appropriate separation needs. In summary, be patient when your child presents some mild to moderate symptoms of distress. Give them a chance, with your loving support, to work through their stressors. You will recognize your child's need for professional help. We can't protect our children from disappointment, fears, and failure. We can be there to nurture, teach, and assist.

One last remark on this issue of zealous parents rushing their children to therapy. It's the issue of divorce. I'll call these parents, "divorce driven guilt" moms and dads. The parents feel responsible for disrupting the security of their kids. Understandable, but not always the case with their kids. Yes, children suffer when their parents get a divorce, but not all suffer to the extent that professional therapy is required. Most kids have extended family structures that supply solace, understanding, and support to the children as they cope with the separation and divorce of their parents. Remember, children are resilient. Not all kids in a divorce situation need psychotherapy, but what most will need is time to get accustomed to the changes that will result from divorce. I've had parents who brought their kids to therapy immediately upon the initial rumbling of a dysfunctional spousal relationship, and the children demonstrated no symptoms of distress. I guess the message is to be patient with the child's adjustment, and don't assume they won't be able to cope. Also, some children demonstrate "delayed" reaction to family turmoil. Be vigilant, but not over-reactive.

> Neurotics build castles in the sky,
> Psychotics live in them,
> Psychiatrists collect the rent.

Chapter 7: How to Obtain Referrals and What to do Next

Obtaining referrals and how to act upon them: A check list follows.

Ask your personal physician for at least two, preferably three, recommended names of licensed mental health providers. Inquire if he received any feedback from the patients he knew that completed therapy with the recommended therapists.

- Ask a trusted family member or friend who may have knowledge of psychotherapists in your city for recommendations. It is not necessary to divulge your reasons for seeking therapy, unless you have full trust in sharing a confidence with the person.

- If you are a member of a church, ask your clergy for a recommendation. Most priests, ministers, rabbis and other church leaders make contacts with therapists in their communities. They frequently counsel their members and are aware of when their parishioners require professional care.
- If your need for counseling may lead to a legal/court issue (separation from a spouse/divorce, child custody, personal injury, disability determination, wrongful job termination, sexual harassment at work, etc.) ask several attorneys for recommendations for a psychotherapist experienced in these areas. (You also may wish to inquire of the mental health provider, her experience with testifying in a court of law.) Attorneys often refer their clients to mental health providers.
- Look in the yellow pages, under the headings of Psychiatrists, Psychologists, Social Workers, and Psychotherapists. *Caution: Only licensed psychologists, psychiatrists, and social workers can advertise under their respective titles. An unlicensed therapist can be listed*

under the general term, "psychotherapist." Persons with a designation of Licensed Professional Counselor (LPC) are licensed to provide general counseling, and may be listed as psychotherapists. There will also be categories in the yellow pages of "marriage counseling" or "family counseling" that may or may not be licensed. When calling a listing in the phone book, one should ascertain whether the person is licensed or holds certification by a state governing board. If not licensed, proceed to the next name.

- Some communities have agencies that are called "referral agencies." These agencies will have lists of professionals in the community. Call your local mental heath association, school board, or agencies such as Alcoholics Anonymous (AA), Gamblers Anonymous (GA) or Overeaters Anonymous.
- Larger general hospitals will often have psychology or psychiatry units, and they can provide the names of licensed psychotherapists who perform out-patient treatment. Inpatient psychiatry and chemical dependency hospitals can be helpful in providing names of their mental health professional resources.

- If you are trying to find a therapist for your child or teenager, talk to your pediatrician, your child's elementary or high school counselor, the local school board's Special Education Services Department, or other parents you know who have procured psychotherapy for their children.
- If your insurance is a managed care provider or an Employee Assistance Program (EAP), they will have a list of qualified providers. From their referral base, get the names and start your calls to speak to them. Don't just accept one provider name and schedule an appointment.

What to do next? Make some phone calls.

Now you have some names, addresses, and phone numbers of potential psychotherapists in front of you. Find a comfortable chair, pick up the phone and start your calling. Expect to be told that the doctor is in session, or unavailable at the moment and what is the nature of your call (who knows, you may be fortunate to speak to the therapist immediately). By all means, tell the receptionist or office manager that you are considering scheduling an appointment but you wish to speak to the therapist before you do. Let them know when you will be available for a return call. Be pleasant and polite. Then go on to the next name.

Some suggestions on what to ask the therapist.

Hopefully, you received several therapists' return calls from your referral list. Those, who choose not to return your calls within 48 hours, I would scratch off your list. I always returned the calls from clients who clearly identified their need to speak with me prior to scheduling an appointment. It was my belief that the person wanted to know some things about my training, experience in working with their issues, office practices, etc., and that signaled to me a person who was motivated and serious about treatment. The calls to these prospective clients also provided me with important information that was incorporated into their intake-initial session. Additionally, a degree of rapport was established even before meeting the person, face-to-face. It is most important that you feel comfortable with your therapist, and the phone contact can start this process of evaluating your "comfort barometer." Now, let's get to the questions you might want to ask, *before* you agree to see the therapist.

You have the psychotherapist on the phone. Thank the therapist for returning your call. Introduce yourself, and indicate that you are trying to find a therapist that would be best suited to you and the issues you believe are troubling you. Give a brief account of your troubling concerns.

State that you have some questions that you would like to ask to assist in making a choice of a therapist. Below are some questions to ask:

1. "Are you a licensed professional therapist (psychologist, psychiatrist, social worker), and number of years in practice? Are you in a solo (private) or group practice?" Ask about training received and additional credentials.

2. "Would you please tell me what you consider to be your major therapy approach or orientation, such as psychoanalytic, behaviorist, cognitive, humanistic or eclectic?"

3. Briefly described what you think are your concerns (depression, anxiety, eating disorder, trying to decide to stay or exit my marriage, or any other issue.

Then ask, "What is your experience in working with this type of problem?"

4. "What is your professional fee? Do you charge more for the initial office visit?

How long is an individual session? I have private insurance. Will your office file the insurance forms for me? Will you accept my co-pay, and wait until the insurance pays the balance? I'm enrolled in a managed care program at work, and your name was provided to me. Did you have a good experience with working with my insurance plan? What is your policy on missed appointments?"

5. "Relative to my perceived issues, does your therapy approach provide for brief therapy?"

6. "Do you work with my age group?

7. "Do you have group therapy available in

your practice?"
You may have many more questions, but the above should provide a good basis of important information to make a judgment of whether she is the right therapist for you. If you have questions about spirituality, values, your sexual orientation concerns, confidentially and other issues, you might want to wait and address them in person at the initial session.

The phone contact should provide you with a "good feel" about the therapist. If it doesn't, go to the next name on your list. Remember it is your therapy, and you need to feel positive about the person with whom you will be working in this important relationship.

After you are in the therapy process, continue to assess your rapport with your therapist. If you begin to feel uncomfortable about an issue, bring it up with the therapist and discuss it. Don't leave things unresolved when it comes to your comfort level. Tell your therapist your thoughts and feelings. I can recall on many occasions, when clients asked for clarification about an issue in the therapy process that caused them some concern, and in almost all cases, was easily resolved. This will tend to strengthen the therapist-client alliance. Remember, the quality of the therapist-client relationship is very much related to your therapy outcome.

Chapter 8: Conclusion / "Bailing Hay"

One of my professors at the University of Oklahoma use to say after hours of covering course material, discussion, and debate, "We have cut a lot of hay, let's bale some." I have attempted to cover many issues that would assist you in selecting the right therapist *before* you enter therapy, and some issues for you to consider *during* the process of therapy. I tried to utilize the experience I gained in working with the first-time client. Any time we try something new, it can be somewhat intimidating, and we may have many questions lurking within us, but not the "know how" of what to ask. Many times we say to ourselves, "I wish I would have asked this or that, before I got myself into this situation."

While it is never too late for clarification, it would probably be better to know before you make an important decision such as selecting the appropriate psychotherapist. I think, after reading this, you will be a more knowledgeable client, and possibly enhance a more effective outcome through psychotherapy. In the spirit of "baling hay," let's look at some of the salient issues brought out in this book, and put them into easy reference or summary styles.

Important "Bales of Hay" covered in this book.

Salient point #1: Mental health professionals come with different training; consequently there should be no assumption that they have equal qualifications to treat mental health conditions. It is prudent to be familiar with their training so you can choose your therapist based upon your perceived needs.

Salient point #2: The orientations or types of psychotherapy vary significantly, in theory and in application. After reading this book, it is hoped that you have gained an appreciation for the different approaches mental health providers may use in treatment. Remember, many therapists are trained in several of the orientations, and an eclectic approach may be available. It is important that you feel comfortable with the type of therapy focus directed to your emotional, behavioral and cognitive problems.

Salient point #3: Therapy can occur in

individual, group, couples, or family formats.

Individual therapy is the most frequently used format, but group, couples, and family formats are equally important to the healing process. On occasion, a client may be enrolled in individual as well as in couples, or group or family therapies. Play therapy is most appropriate for children, as it lends itself to the best format for the communication effort with the child. Through play activities, structured and unstructured, a child will be best apt to relate their emotional and behavioral issues.

Salient point #4: Psychological testing, or diagnostics, can play an important role in your therapy.

It may be helpful in determining your diagnosis, and the direction for treatment. I provided information on several standardized instruments that are used to measure various traits of which you should have familiarity. Psychological testing may or may not be incorporated in your treatment regiment.

Salient point #5: You will be given a diagnosis. It is important you understand the diagnoses provided and how it was generated. The explanations will allow you to be privy in understanding diagnostic classifications. You are entitled to know this information.

Salient point #6: Your rights concerning confidentiality, privacy and privileges in psychotherapy are important to understand so trust in the therapy process can be assured. You also need to be aware of the exceptions noted that mandate disclosure of therapy content. Other issues were noted and should be discussed with your therapist if you have concerns.

Salient point #7: Children and adolescents are not "miniature adults." When they suffer significant distress and require psychotherapy, the right therapist for your kid is critically important. Characteristics needed in the child/adolescent therapist are listed, along with what parents should expect in their initial consult with their child's therapist. What to ask the therapist was discussed. Kids on medication are discussed and a most informative book was introduced. Caution should be exercised for over zealous parents who rush their children into therapy, not appreciating the resilience of children to cope.

Salient point #8: The payment of fees by your insurance carrier, or your managed care provider must be understood at the onset of therapy. Clarifying money issues are important to established so it will not create any tension in the therapy process. Special concerns for confidentiality in filing insurance and managed care claims were discussed.

Salient point #9: General guidelines for ethics in psychotherapy were discussed. It is the responsibility of the therapist to keep abreast of current and any future modifications of the ethical statues of the American Psychological Association and other governing agencies. The discussion of boundaries in the client-therapist relationship was limited to the major concerns, and what response a therapist should make when there is concern that a violation has occurred.

Salient point #10: You may have been recommended for therapy by your physician or another professional, and several referral psychotherapists' names may have been provided. If you decide to seek therapy and need a referral, how do you go about this process? The suggestions given in this book will help you achieve this daunting task.

Salient point #11: Once you have some names of psychotherapists, it is important to make a phone contact prior to making an appointment. Questions to ask your potential therapist were outlined, and are considered by this author as very important and need to be *answered before* you schedule an appointment. Don't schedule your child or teen until you have a positive intuitive feeling toward the therapist.

Salient point #12: Don't overlook your participation in support groups in conjunction with your individual, couples or group psychotherapies. Chapter10, provides a good starting list of many agencies, cites for information, and support groups.

Salient point #13: The book in its entirety, offers you an opportunity to clear up the murky waters of psychotherapy. I attempted to provide you with a clear, concise, and a readable journey into achieving positive mental health. I kept the terminology to the basic minimal, without compromising what I believed will benefit you in your journey to selecting the right psychotherapist.

Let's wrap this up.

I've tried to keep this short and to the point. I sense that people who seek an intelligent process to choosing a psychotherapist do not want to read a book for hours and hours. I tried to focus on what you would benefit from *before* you start your psychotherapy and a little during your therapy journey. I hope I've been successful.

Your therapy can be a major life-changing event, or it can be a waste of your time and money. Your preparation for selecting the right therapist, and the right therapy-orientation, can increase your chances for a positive outcome. A little thought and guided direction are worth the effort. I know I would have been delighted to have *all* my clients possess the information contained in these pages. When I've seen other mental health providers in therapy (yes, they have issues too), they were able to assist in the treatment process due to having the same knowledge that was shared in this book. Having a therapy alliance with someone, who demonstrates their willingness to learn, is a delight for the therapist. Effective therapy begins in securing the right therapist for you, and your dependents, and the therapeutic relationship must be one that encompasses the appropriate therapy orientation.

You can read parts of this book again and

again, and keep it as a reference during your on-going therapy experience. If, in reading, you develop positive attitudes toward one or more therapy orientations, I encourage you to read from the short list of references provided. Each book will generate more references.

Lagniappe

I live in south Louisiana, in the heart of "Cajun Country." Cajuns found refuge in Louisiana after British forces exiled them from Acadia, their homeland on the Atlantic Coast of Canada, in the mid-18th century. These are hard working, friendly, and charitable people. One of the customs of the Cajuns is to offer a "gift" or "something extra" to others, called "lagniappe." So in the spirit of "lagniappe," allow me to offer to you a little something extra, "mon ami."

People seek psychotherapy in the hope of relieving emotional pain and resolving conflicts within themselves, and with others. They wish to change dysfunctional habits into more appropriate, functional behaviors, ones that will not cause stress. They want to rid themselves of depression, eating disorders, anxiety and, as paraded in this book, our fallible nature as human beings. Psychotherapy equates with change, changes in our thinking, feeling and behaviors. In most cases, with the right therapist, and a motivated client, change will occur. The responsibility to maintain the positive changes lies with the client. I've had clients who returned to therapy after six-months or longer, complaining of a re-emergence of the original dysfunctions. Upon examination, it was established that they stopped using the "lessons" of their previous therapy. The gains in therapy must be practiced until they have become integrated into the very essence of the "new psychic." Old dysfunctional habits can easily sneak back into our pattern of daily life. One must continue to practice, instill, and be vigilant of what you achieved in therapy.

Another issue needs to be addressed for the reader. It may be perceived with a cautionary tone. I have often received clients who desired therapy for marital issues or for a couple issue. However, his or her mates chose or refused to come to couples therapy. This sets up an interesting scenario. When only one spouse or mate in a troubled relationship receives psychotherapy, growth and change of the client, may leave the absent mate "out of the loop." In fact, the healthy changes may expose the absent mate to feeling threatened and insecure. For example, if the mate who is receiving therapy presents a passive and non-assertive approach in expressing his/her needs, and is taught assertive skills, the absent-from-therapy mate may not appreciate the change. A power struggle may arise or the client may begin to evaluate his/her desire to stay in the relationship. I've received calls from husbands, wives, and lovers who expressed distress and even anger with the changes they noted in their mate's therapy involvement. In essence, they did not want to see any change in the relationship. Of course, I couldn't discuss their mate's therapy, but could only invite them into couple's therapy, if their mate consented. The same issues are also noted in family counseling when one or more family members refused to become involved. Therapy, in most cases, results in change for the benefit of the client and, if it involves a relationship, it is best to have all parties represented.

Another lagniappe. Your psychotherapist must keep your confidentiality rights protected. You may tell others about your therapy, but the therapist can't. She will guard your privilege of privacy. It doesn't really matter if you received therapy in towns of 50,000 populations or in cities of 500,000 or greater, you may see your therapist in the mall, a restaurant, or a concert. She may be with her husband, or friends. If you approach her and say more then a "good evening Dr. Therapist," you may have said too much. I've had clients approach me with my wife and friends, and proceed to discuss their therapy, or tell my companions how much I've helped them. This is not appropriate. It places your therapist in a compromising position of protecting your privacy. A wave in her direction and a nod of recognition is appropriate. Your therapist can't be your social friend. I hope I was not too blunt, but sometimes clients want to dissolve the necessary boundaries in the therapist-client professional relationship. Who knows, you may want to re-enter therapy with the same therapist years after your therapy was completed. Thus, your professional relationship with the therapist must be maintained.

A final lagniappe. Most professionals are willing, to a limited degree, to provide their services, gratis, (free of charges) or at a reduced fee. If you are without insurance and have limited funds for counseling, ask the therapist if she is willing to adjust her fees. If she can't, she can most likely provide you with sources in your community to meet your financial limitation. Don't be hesitant to ask.

Good luck to you. I wish you positive mental health.

Before we get to the references, let's have a final joke or two.

A psychologist is at a party talking with a small group of people, when a man comes up behind him and taps him on the shoulder. The psychologist turns around and the man hauls off and decks him. The psychologist gets up, brushes himself off, turns to the group and declares, "That's his problem."

Two psychologists meet at their twentieth college reunion. One of them looks like he just graduated, while the other psychologist looks old, worried and withered.
The older looking one asks the other, "What's your secret?" Listening to other people's problems every day, all day long, for years on end, has made an old man of me."
The younger looking one replies,
"Who listens?"

Chapter 9: References and Comments

As promised, listed are a few references that you might want to read. I have identified each as relative to the four major schools of psychotherapy orientations: Psychoanalytic (psychodynamic), Behaviorist, Cognitive, and Humanistic.

Obviously, hundreds of references can be found in each of the major therapy approaches relative to their theories and applications.

Psychoanalytic

Gaylin, (M.D.) Willard, (2001) *How Psychotherapy Really Works: How It Works When It Works and Why Sometimes It Doesn't.* New

York: Contemporary Books (Division of McGraw-Hill). (ISBN: 0-8092-9475-3)

Dr. Gaylin is a physician (psychiatrist), trained in psychoanalysis, and writes a wonderful book, in a compassionate style, as he addresses many issues in the therapist/patient relationship. His contemporary take on psychoanalysis is understandable to the layman. He provides the reader with a good look into the vast complexity of hidden motives, the complexity of the unconscious, and what is necessary for therapy to work. The reader, who finds merit in the psychodynamic approach, will find reading this book, delightful.

Behaviorism

Skinner, B. F. (1976) *About Behaviorism.* New York: Random House, Inc. (ISBN: 0394716183*)*

The basics of theory and application by one of the masters of behaviorism philosophy.

Cognitive

Beck, Judith S. (Foreword by Aaron T. Beck) (1995) *Cognitive Therapy: Basics and Beyond,* New York: Guilford Publications, Inc. (ISBN: 0898628474)

This book is written by Aaron Beck's daughter, and provides an excellent foundation to the concepts of cognitive theory and treatment processes. It is an introductory text that outlines a foundation in the central principles and treatment methods of cognitive therapy.

Ellis, Ellis, & Harper, Robert A. (1975) *A New Guide to Rational Living,* Hollywood, California, Wilshire Book Company (ISBN: 0-87980-042-9)

This book presents a direct and bold explanation of Rational Emotive Therapy (RET) philosophy and methodology within the cognitive model. Ellis and Harper strongly make their case that this therapy works. I have had many on my clients read this book, and they came away challenged in their efforts to confront their irrational beliefs.

Blau, Shawn (Editor) (1998) *The Albert Ellis Reader: A Guide to Well-Being Using Rational Emotive Behavior Therapy*, Carol Publishing Group, New Jersey (ISBN: 0806520329)

Edited by Shawn Blau, with updates by E. Ellis, contains thirty (30) of Dr. Ellis' articles, on numerous issues that he addresses in his bold and frank manner. It covers topics of romance, sex, anger, work, and many other issues that make-up our existence.

Humanism

Rogers, Carl R. (Adapted by A.D. Yalom) (1995) *On Becoming a Person: A Therapist View of Psychotherapist,* Boston, Houghton Mifflin Company. (ISBN:039575531X) This book revisits the work of Carl Rogers, founder of the humanistic movement, and client-centered therapy. His work on personal growth and creativity is re-introduced.

Thorne, Brain (1992) (republished in 2003)

Carl Rogers, Thousand Oaks, California, SAGE Publications.(ISBN: 0761941118)

This book, republished in 2003, presents Rogers' basic theories, and his ideals of therapeutic intervention. Actual procedures of his treatments with clients are documented. You will gain a true sense and feel of the humanistic methodology used by Carl Rogers.

Frankl, Viktor E. (c.1939, 1963) *Man's Search for Meaning,* New York, Pocket Books, Simon & Schuster.(ISBN: 0-671-45462-5). I have read this book at least three times during and after my graduate studies, and have recommended it to countless clients. As a psychiatrist, and a prisoner in a Nazi concentration camp, Dr. Frankl developed Logotherapy, or existential analysis. After reading this little book, I bet you will want to reflect on your life. When we find a "why" (purpose) to our existence, we can put up with any "how" (circumstance) we exist. I remind myself of this truth everyday.

Brief Therapy

Budman, S. H., Gurman, A. S. (1988) *Theory and Practice of Brief Therapy,* New York, Guilford Press. (ISBN:0-89862-716-8) Written primarily for the professional therapist, I believe that anyone who reads the book will gain significant insight to the history, development and research on brief therapy. Well organized and written.

Diagnostic Strategy

American Psychiatric Association, *Diagnostic and Statistical Manual of Mental Disorders, DSM-IV, 4th Edition,* Copyright 1994, Washington, D.C. The ultimate guide to provide diagnoses. Available to the public. A good resource for those who have received psychotherapy and want to know more about how they were diagnosed.

Children on Psychiatric Medications

Wilens, Timothy E., *Straight Talk About Psychiatric Medication for Kids,* revised edition, The Guilford Press, New York, c2004, ISBN: 1-59385-031-x) This book is a must read for any parent who has concerns, questions, and needs to understand the process of kids on psychiatric medication. Dr. Wilens does a great service to educate parents on this topic. Easy to read and understand. He explains all medical terms. He also demonstrates a true sense of compassion and empathy for parents, who face the issue of medication to treat psychiatry disorders of their children. I wish this book was available when I was in practice. It should provide much clarity for parents.

Mental Health Jokes

The jokes included in this book were found on various web sites. When the author of the joke was provided, credit was given. Most of the jokes had no author cited.

Don't overlook Chapter 10 that provides you with some important resources to get started on your educational preparation for psychotherapy!

Chapter 10: Resources: Where to Find Help

"Let your fingers start the education process."

This chapter presents only a partial list of national agencies and other resource links that provide helpful information. I've selected ones that will get you started. As you know, each resource will lead you to tens of other similar websites and agencies. Aren't computers and the internet wonderful? The resources provided incorporates national associations offering general information, brochures, books on a broad spectrum of dysfunctions, with a phone number, many of them toll-free, a physical address, and/or web address. Additionally, I have provided specific agencies that offer help for specific disorders. Most provide a no-fee support group. I believe, that prior to your first schedule appointment, you, a family member or your friend, should learn as much as possible about the disorders you believe are creating distress in your life. The more you know, the more viable a client you will be, as well as having a clearer direction in selecting the appropriate therapist. Your therapist will be impressed with the knowledge you bring to your first session. Support groups are invaluable to your individual, couples or group therapies. I hope you find the following resources useful.

NATIONAL AGENCIES FOR GENERAL INFORMATION

National Institute of Mental Health (NIMH)

A general source to obtain information on all the psychological/psychiatric disorders that are found in the *Diagnostic and Statistical Manual of Mental Disorders* previously referenced in this book. Quoting from their webpage, NIMH, "provides state-of-the-art mental health information to the public, media, Congress, voluntary and advocacy groups, interest groups, students, educators, and scientists."

Toll Free 1-866-615-6464;
Email: nimhinfo@nih.gov;
Website: www.nimh.nih.gov

National Mental Health Association (NMHA).--- This resource and referral center "serves people seeking mental health information for themselves, family members or friends, provides guidance on how to become an advocate for mental health rights and general resources for professionals." Single copy of brochures are available upon request, and downloadable fact sheets on more than 60 mental health topics; referrals to more than 6000 treatment centers support groups and national organizations, staffed by trained professionals, while they will *not* offer medical/ legal advice, or counseling, they can provide referrals to other organizations that offer these services.

Mailing Address:
National Mental Health Assoc.,
2001 N. Beauregard St., 12th Floor,
Alexandria, Virginia 22311
Toll Free 1-800-969-NMHA (6642)

If you need immediate help, call the National Hopeline Network 1-800-SUICIDE (1-800-784-2433) Website: www.nmha.org

National Alliance on Mental Illness (NAMI)

"NAMI is the nation's largest grassroots mental health organization dedicated to improving the lives of persons living with serious mental illness and their families. Found in every state, and in 1100 local communities across the nation, work together through research, support, advocacy, and education." It is also a referral agency.

Mailing Address:
National Alliance on Mental Illness
2107 Wilson Blvd.,
Suite 300, Arlington, VA 22201-304
Helpline: 1-800-950-6264;
Website www.nami.org

Anxiety Disorders Association of America (ADAA)

"The ADAA is the only national, non-profit association solely dedicated to informing the public, professional, and legislators that anxiety disorders are real, serious and treatable." ADAA provides educational information and resources on treatment providers to those in need. The association will assist in developing self-help skills.

Mailing Address:
Anxiety Disorders Association of America
8730 Georgia Ave, Suite 600,
Silver Springs, MD 20910
Phone: (240) 485-1001,
Web Address: www.adaa.org

American Psychological Association
www.apa.org;
Phone:1-800-374-2721
American Psychiatric Association
www.psych.org;
Phone: 1-703-907-7300

Both organizations offer information on mental disorders, contact sources, books, and a variety of other services. Please note that the American Psychological Assoc. is comprised of academics and practicing psychologists involved in research and treatment studies, and the American Psychiatric Assoc. is comprised of medical specialists.

U.S. Department of Health and Human Services

www.os.dhhs.gov

Phone: 1-887-696-6775

A major agency within the United States, dedicated to "better health, safety and well being."

Provides information on diseases, inclusive of mental health, safety and wellness, drug and food information, families and children, aging health issues, domestic violence and child abuse, smoking and drinking.

National Suicide Prevention Hotline

www.suicidepreventionlifeline.org

Toll Free: 1-800-273-8225 (TALK)

The only national suicide prevention and intervention telephone resource funded by the federal government. By reaching the above number, you will be connected to the nearest available suicide prevention and treatment provider.

DRUG AND ALCOHOL ABUSE and/or ADDICTION

SAMHSA'S NCADI www.health.org/research

This is an online library collection, one of the largest repositories of alcohol and drug use information in the world, offers internet access to current literature, research reports, and educational resources.

Alcoholics Anonymous (AA) www.alcoholics-anonymous.org

Phone: 212-870-3400

A fellowship of adult women and men whose main goal is to stop drinking, utilizing the Twelve-Step Program. There are no dues or fees for membership. You can find a group meeting in your community, just by looking in your phone book.

Alcoholics Anonymous for Families (AL-Anon) www.al-anon.org

Phone: 1-888-425-2666

Alcoholism is a family disease, estimated to affect at least four other people, whether they are drinking or not. This program offers education and support to families.

Alcoholics Anonymous for Teens (Alateen) www.alateen.org

Phone: 1-888-425-2666

A program for the younger members of a family affected by problem drinking or alcoholism. Again, a Twelve-Step Program that offers support.

National Association for Children of Alcoholics

www.nacoa.net

Phone: 1-888-554-2627

Quoting their web-page, "A place where you can: learn how alcohol and other drugs hurt everyone in a family; learn how to feel safer and less stressed out; find new ways to deal with hassles at home and find hope, even if your parents don't change."

Adult Children of Alcoholics

www.adultchildren.org

Phone: 310-534-1815

Email: acaabc@earthlink.net

This is also a Twelve Step Program for men and women who grew up in an alcoholic home and experienced the dysfunctions usually associated to alcoholic abuse and addiction. This organization will assist you in finding a meeting in or near your community.

Alcohol and Drug Abuse Hotline

1-800-Alcohol (252-6465)

This toll free number connects to a national referral service that will put you in touch with providers through-out the nation for treatment of alcohol and drug abusers and addicts.

Cocaine Hotline
1-800-Cocaine (262-2463)

Another toll-free hotline that will provide you with information and referrals across the nation on cocaine abuse and addiction.

Narcotics Anonymous (NA)
www.na.org
1-800-777-1515

"Narcotics Anonymous is an international, community based association of recovering drug addicts with more than 33,500 weekly meetings in over 116 countries worldwide," according to its website. Membership is available to men and women with drug addiction, regardless of the drug or combination of drugs. Since it grew out of Alcoholics Anonymous, it utilizes the same Twelve-Step Program.

Nicotine Anonymous
www.nicotine-anonymous.org
Email: info@nicotine-anonymous.org
Phone: 1-877-879-4762

This is a Twelve-Step fellowship of men and women who help each other to lead a nicotine-free life-style. The program is free, meets weekly, provides information, and support about the mental and emotional aspects of quitting all tobacco products.

GAMBLING ADDICTION
Gamblers Anonymous (GA)
www.gamblersanonymous.org
Email: isomain@gamblersanonymous.org
Address: GA, P.O. Box 17173, Los Angeles, CA 90017

Based on the AA Twelve-Step Program, offers a self-help method through regular group meetings for support on addiction and learning responsibility on money matters. One of its web-pages helps you to locate GA meeting in your state and community.

National Council on Problem Gambling, Inc.
www.ncpgambling.org
Phone: 1-800-522-4700

Offers a 24- hour hotline, provide information, educational and referrals for treatment.

Gam-Anon/Gam-A-Teen
www.gam-anon.org
Phone: 718-352-1671

Support groups for family and friends of a problem gambler, based on the Twelve-Step AA Program.

CHILD AND ADOLESCENT ISSUES

The Child Advocate
www.childadvocate.net
Email: **exp32@yahoo.com**

The Child Advocate is a not-for-profit, national network, devoted to children, parents and for professionals who work with them. This site offers legal/court advocacy, educational/school advocacy, and medical/psychiatric advocacy. While not offering advice or counseling, The Child Advocate will offer information through links and groups that will provide services to your child or family. The professional staff is entirely volunteer and receives no payment for their services.

Children and Adults with Attention Deficient Disorder (CHADD)
www.chadd.org
Phone: 1-800-233-4050
Address:
CHADD
8181 Professional Place
Suite 150,
Landover, MD 20785

CHADD is the nation's largest non-profit organization helping individuals with AD/HD and their families. With over 16,000 members, and 200 local chapters, offers support for individuals, parents, teachers, and professionals. CHADD, in response to the frustration and sense of isolation experienced by parents and their children with AD/HD, this organization has been received well.

Child and Adolescent Bipolar Foundation (CABF)
www.cabf.org
Address:
CABF
1000 Skokie Blvd., Suite 425,
Wilmette, Il 60091

Membership is for parents, guardians, and others caring for children with bipolar disorder. Professional membership for those who provide treatment for bipolar children is also available.

Both groups provide support, information, linking parents to resources; provide counsel on medications, and alternative treatment approaches. On-line support groups are available.

Depression and Bipolar Support Alliance (DBSA)
www.DBSAlliance.org
Phone: 1-800 826-3632
Address:
DBSA,
730 N. Franklin St., Suite 501,
Chicago, Il 60610-7224

DBSA is a not-for-profit organization that responds to 5,000 calls per month on the toll free information and referral line. Information packets, free of charge, are available to anyone requesting information about mood disorders. Over 100,000 individuals visit their website each month. Their mission is to ensure that people of all ages with mood disorders are treated equitably.

Families for Depression Awareness
www.familyaware.org
Email: info@familyaware.org
Address:
Families for Depression Awareness,
300 Fifth Ave., Waltham, MA 02451
Phone: (781) 487-0009

This site provides information about depression, medical help, support groups, and books. Offers counsel on how to help a depressed person seek treatment, and information on how to prevent suicide. Additionally, it teaches how to recognize your stressors as caretaker of a depressed family member. Information on childhood, adolescent and adult depression is provided, as well as reports on the most current research findings.

Tourette's Syndrome Association (TSA)
www.tsa-usa.org
Phone: 718-224-2999,
Toll Free:1-888-4-touret,
Address:
Tourette's Syndrome Association, Inc. (TS),
42-40 Bell Blvd., Bayside, N.Y. 11361

TS is a neurological disorder in early childhood or adolescent between the ages of 2 and 15, with defined symptoms of multiple motor and vocal tics. This association has a national membership fee of $45.00 per year, which includes your local chapter and entitles you to the TSA website/newsletter, referral lists for medical, psychological, lawyers, and other advocates for persons with TS. Two full-time information and referral staff members help you with your inquires. There are other benefits of membership. Check out this website.

Autism Society of America
www.autism-society.org
Address:
Autism Society of America
7910 Woodmont Ave., Suite 300,
Bethesda, Maryland, 20814-3067
Phone: 1-800328-8476

While not providing direct services such as treatment or legal services, they provide information and referrals to numerous services available for autism.

National Center for Children Exposed to Violence
www.nccev.org
Phone: 877-496-2238
Email: nccev@info.med.yale.edu
Address:
Child Study Center

230 South Frontage Rd.,
P.O. Box 207900
New Haven, CT 06520

A primary national source for anyone desiring information about the effects of violence exposure on children can be found here. The center will provide literature, Internet resources and a bibliographic database and will respond to inquires for information on the most promising programs related to children exposed to violence.

TeenScreen
www.teenscreen.org
Phone: 866-833-6727
Email: teenscreen@childpsych.columbia.edu

According to this website, 750,000 teens suffer from depression, some so acute, it leads to suicide, the third leading cause of adolescent death. The TeenScreen program offers parents the opportunity for their teens to receive a voluntary mental health check-up, inclusive of symptoms of mental illness, suicide risk, in a safe and confidential manner. The program offers both paper and pencil and computerized screening tools. This site will assist you in starting a local community program.

SOS High School Suicide Prevention Program
www.mentalhealthscreening.org
Email: smhinfo@mentalhealthscreening.org
Address:

Screening for Mental Health (SMH), Inc.,
One Washington St., Suite 304,
Wellesley Hills, MA 02481

SMH programs now include online screening (as well as in person) programs for depression, bipolar disorder, generalized anxiety disorder, post-traumatic stress disorder, eating disorders, alcohol problems, and suicide prevention.

National Center for Learning Disabilities (NCLD)

www.ld.org
Phone 1-888-575-7373
Address:
National Center for Learning Disabilities,
381 Park Avenue South, Suite 1401,
New York, N.Y. 10016

NCLD provides comprehensive information to parents, professionals, individuals (children, adolescents and adults) with learning disabilities, promotes research and advocacy for educational programs and the rights of the learning disabled.

National Down Syndrome Congress (NDSC)
www.ndsccenter.org
Phone:1-800-232-6372
Address:
NDSC,
1370 Center Drive, Suite 102,
Atlanta, GA 30338

Provides up-to-date information on Down

Syndrome, publishes six times a year, a newsletter providing information on resources on programs and services available to people with Down Syndrome and the appropriateness of the programs. It is a national clearinghouse on Down Syndrome.

Teens Living with Cancer
www.teenslivingwithcancer.org
Phone: 585-334-0858
Address:
245 Citation Dr., Henrietta, NY 14467

A wonderful website for general and specific information about teens coping with cancer. In the language for young people, it covers all medical, psychological, educational, and spiritual dimensions for teens to deal with their cancer.

National Foundation for Abused and Neglected Children (NFANC)
www.gangfreekids.org
Emails: For Child Abuse Info:
nfanc@hotmail.com
For Juvenile Justice Info:
gangfreee99@hotmail.com
Address:
NFANC,
P.O. Box 1841,
Chicago, IL 60660-1841

NFANC is a non-profit agency for abuse and neglected children that produces various publications, program materials, and policy reports.

If contacted, they will provide information on short courses, seminars, and workshops with the goal of preventing child abuse and neglect.

EATING DISORDERS
Overeaters Anonymous (OA)
www.overeatersanonymous.org
Phone: 505-891-2664
Email: info@oa.org
Address:
World Service Office,
P.O. Box 44020
Rio Rancho, NM 87174

OA offers a Twelve-Step, self-help support program for compulsive overeating. It is not just about weight lost, but addresses physical, emotional and spiritual well-being. Encourages its members to develop a food plan, consult with a health professional and obtain a sponsor.

National Association of Anorexia Nervosa and Associated Disorders (ANAD)
www.anad.org
Phone:
ANAD Hotline: 847-831-3438
Address:
ANAD,
P.O. Box 7,
Highland Park, IL 60035

NADA offers a national hotline, free support groups throughout the United States, referrals to health care professionals, education and prevention programs, for anorexia, bulimia and compulsive overeating individuals.

Obsessive Compulsive Foundation (OCF)
www.ocfoundation.org
Phone: 203-401-2070
Email: info@ocfoundation.org
Address:
OCF,
676 State St.
New Haven, CT 06511

I decided to put this resource under the Eating Disorders section for obvious reasons.

Obsessive ideation and compulsive behaviors of individuals with eating dysfunction are well documented. This foundation is non-profit, international, and was formed by a group of individuals with OCD, and dedicated to educating the public, support services, and providing a list of professionals that treat persons with OCD and related disorders. Bi-monthly newsletters are offered to its members.

SEXUAL DISORDERS
Sex Addicts Anonymous (SAA)
www.sexaa.org
Phone: 1-800477-1891
Email: info@saa-recovery.org
Address:
SAA,
P.O. Box 70949
Houston, TX 77270

This is a membership for men and women, who support each other in their effort to overcome their sexual addictions and dependency. Based upon the program for Alcoholics Anonymous, SAA is supported by voluntary contributions.

Sex and Love Addicts Anonymous (SLAA)
www.slaafws.org
Phone: 781-255-8825
Email: info@slaafws.org
Address:
Fellowship-Wide Services,
P.O. Box 338,
Norwood, Massachusetts 02062

No fee for the participants, but will accept contributions. Again, a program based on the Twelve-Step process of AA. Open to both genders, which support each other in their addictions to sex and love, with a goal of maintaining a healthy commitment to a relationship.

SEXUAL ABUSE VICTIMS:

Survivors of Incest Anonymous World Service Office, Inc.

www.siawso.org

Phone: (Hotline) 410-893-3322

Email: feedback@siawso.org

Address:

SIAWSO,

P.O. Box 190,

Benson, MD 21018-9998

A support group for men and women, 18 years and older who are survivors of child sexual abuse (incest) and as a victim are not abusing any child. Incest is defined broadly, inclusive of extended family members, as well as other trusted adults (teacher, coach, clergy, step-parent, etc.

Based on the concepts of AA.

The SaferSociety Foundation, Inc.

www.safersociety.org

Phone: 802-247-3132

Address:

The Safer Society Foundation, Inc.

P.O. Box 340

Brandon, Vermont, 05733

This resource is a non-profit agency and functions as a national research, advocacy, and referral center for the prevention and treatment of sexual abuse. Website will outline all services provided.

AdvocateWeb
www.advocatewev.org
Address:
AdvocateWeb,
P.O. Box 202961
Austin, TX 78720

Quoting from their website, "AdvocateWeb is a nonprofit organization providing information and resources to promote awareness and understanding of the issues involved in the exploitation (emotional/sexual) of persons by trusted helping professionals. We are attempting to be a helpful resource for victims/survivors, their families and friends, the general public, and for victim advocates and professionals."

Rape, Abuse, and Incest National Network
www.rainn.org
Toll free Hotline 1-800-656-4673

Provides a 24- hour hotline which will connect you to the nearest community rape crisis center.

OTHER VARIOUS RESOURCES

Gay and Lesbian National Hotline:
www.glnh.org
Toll-Free Hotline 1-888-843-4564
Email: info@GLBTNationalHelpCenter.org
Youth Talkline: 1-800-246-7743
Address:
GLBT National Help Center,
2261 Marker St.
PMB #296
San Francisco, CA 94114

Please note this website *does not* offer a 24-hour hotline. Calls are received from Monday-to-Friday 6 pm-to-10 pm and Saturday noon-to-5pm, EST. A national, not-for-profit agency, offers peer-counseling, information and referrals for treatment.

National STD (Sexually Transmitted Diseases)
Hotline 1-800-227-8922

Calls are received from Monday-to-Friday, 8 pm-to-11 pm, and is considered an agency of the Centers for Disease Control.

National AIDS Hotline
1-800-342-2437 (AIDS)

Another hotline by the Center for Disease Control. Available 24-hours, provides information and assists in referrals to treatment professions and support group locations, on a national basis.

Parents Anonymous (PA)
www.parentsanonymous.org
Phone: 1-800-421-035; 909-621-6184
Email:
Parentsanonymous@parentsanonymous.org
Address:
PA,
675 West Foothill Blvd.
Suite 220,
Claremont, CA 91711-3475

Provides weekly support meetings, free of charge, and assists in crisis management, and prevention of child abuse by parents. Parents are taught parenting skills, and learn better communication with their children, absent of violence or other abuse issues.

Alzheimer's Disease Education and Referral Center (ADEAR)
www.adaa.org
Phone: 1-800-438-4380
Address:
ADEAR,
P.O. Box 8250
Silver Spring, MD 20907

A United States government funded resource, ADEAR, under the umbrella of the National Institute on Aging, provides information and a referral service. ADEAR further supplies free publications on symptoms, diagnosis, related disorders, risk factors, treatment, care-giving tips. home safety and research.

ToughLove
www.toughlove.org
Phone: 215-348-7090
A support group for parents whose children may demonstrate significant behavioral problems and chemical abuse issues. ToughLove can put parents in touch with local groups, that will assist in teaching coping skills with difficult children.

A similar support group is **Families Anonymous (FA),**
www.familiesanonymous.org
Based on Twelve-Steps of AA, and can be reached at **1-800-736-9805. Address: P.O. 3475, Culver City, CA 90231**

The Association for the Help of Mentally Retarded Children (AHRC)
www.ahrc.org
Phone: 516-626-1000
Requires an annual fee for membership, but the provided services are numerous. Clinical and support help, financial assistance, housing and education are potential services. Focuses on developmental delays and developmental disabilities of individuals.

Recovery, Inc.
www.recovery-inc.com
Phone: 312-337-5661
Email: inquires@recovery-inc.org
Address:
Recovery Inc.
802 N. Dearborn St.
Chicago, IL 60610

A national support program for adults with various psychological symptoms of mood disorders (anxiety and depression), psychotic disorders, including schizophrenia, obsessive-compulsive disorder, personality dysfunctions and other disorders. Members meet to learn coping skills. There is an annual fee, and members receive bimonthly newsletters. Check their website for a location of Recovery, Inc. in your community.

Chapter 11: An Afternoon with a Psychotherapist

If you watch TV, go to plays or movies and read novels, the chances are good you have watched or read a scene of a therapist with a patient. Some of these scenes are accurate depictions of the therapy process; most others come from the creative juices of a screenwriter. Other depictions, frankly, make me angry as a professional psychologist. Yes, I know, in Hollywood or on Broadway, the big studios, and publishers/writers have also taken liberties with other professional men and women, such as attorneys, physicians, CEO's, and even cowboys and Indians. Still, I'm uncomfortable when mental health providers are displayed as psychopathic, unethical, and/or frivolous, seemingly always providing a psychoanalytic model of therapy to the most seriously disturbed patient. Obviously, I get it. The scenes must have drama, significant conflict, and larger than life plots or otherwise it is boring. While "real life" psychotherapy can have the same drama as media psychotherapy, the vast majority of therapeutic efforts by therapists and patients are slow, methodical movements toward resolutions of human mental suffering.

I know at times, with some of my clients, particularly on the first session, they expected me to have some brilliant insight into their problems, and "swoosh", the problem evaporates. If only therapy worked that way!

What follows are four psychotherapy vignettes with four different clients. These are based on real cases, but "fictionalized" to protect the privacy of the clients. I believe it will provide the reader with a "peek" into the therapy process. (I want the reader to respect the process of serious, real therapy, and not be overly-impressed with the therapy scenes of the HBO series, *The "Sopranos"*, the multiple award winning *"Frasier"*, Barbra Streisand in *"The Prince of Tides"*, Bill Murray and Richard Dreyfuss in *"What About Bob"* and who can forget the hilarious movies with Billy Crystal and Robert DeNiro, *"Analyze This"* & "*Analyze That*.")

And so with that introduction, let's take a "voyeuristic" peak into "real psychotherapy."

***

Kevin slumps deep in his chair, gasping for air. He emerges from panic that he describes as "suffocating under a blanket of fear." He holds his head with his hands and finally speaks. "I'm so damn scared, Doc. I feel angry all the time, at what, at whom, I don't know. You understand this? What's the use? I leave my neurotic sweat in this chair and checks with your secretary." Kevin adjusts his six-foot, two-inch frame in the wing-backed chair. He grabs a tissue from the box, and wipes the palms of his hands.

"Don't just stare at me. Tell me how to love myself. Hell, I'll settle for just liking who I am.

So what's the deal with my self-loathing? Why, Doc?" His massive shoulders shake. He may scratch his muscled forearms, leave scars, but he has yet to grieve.

"Take some slow, deep breathes, Kevin."

Clutching the small, soft chair pillow to his stomach, he inhales deeply. His eyes are dark and weary, not menacing, but he remains a fragile, rather gentle man.

"I've lost everyone I wanted to love, and for them to love me. I'm not sure who pushed who away."

Pressing fingers deep into his thighs, Kevin bolts out of the chair and circles the room, "my dad did a number on me, huh, Doc? I couldn't be perfect for the bastard, so I destroyed myself to prove him right. I contaminate people with my anger. You said it before. I don't believe I deserve to be loved."

"Stay with those thoughts, Kevin."

"He wanted me to be the big jock like him. 'You have the size, Kevin, you just don't have the heart,' he told me over and over. Our house was full of his damn trophies, like some high school hero who never outgrows his past." Kevin returns to his chair, strokes the arm rests and breathes deeply.

"I hope he does a slow rot in his grave. All the years he was alive, he never once said he was proud of my grades, my creativity, or my artistic skills. He didn't come to my first sculpture show. And Mom, being the passive, demure wife stayed at home too. Now she's in a nursing home, demented and half the time doesn't know who I am."

"So where do you direct your anger Kevin?"

"I'm not stupid, Doc. I know I do it to myself. Man, I'm so tired of the anger inside of me. Doc, I like my lifestyle, ya know, what I do for a living. My dad use to tell me, more than once, 'only fags do artsy fartsy stuff'. Can you believe that?

"Kevin, maybe you are using your anger at your father to conceal your own non-acceptance of being gay. So, can you truly accept who you are Kevin, without your father's acceptance? He's dead, Kevin, and you will never have it. Remember in a previous session, we identified one of your irrational beliefs. You believe that it's awful, terrible that your father never accepted you for what you are, a talented, bright, kind man who is gay. Until you can change that thought into a more rational belief system, you will stay angry and suffer panic attacks."

"Yes he's dead, he's dead," muffling his deep, painful moans with the chair pillow.

Silence

"I'm exhausted, Doc, can we continue this next week. O.K.?"

Kevin pauses at the door. He returns and picks up the chair pillow, fluffs it, and returns it to its place. As he exits, he smiles like a child who has pleased a parent.

***

"I promised myself I wouldn't cry today," Emily said, already in tears. She grabs a tissue from her large, worn purse, ignoring the box on the table. Her tears fall down her pretty face, void of all makeup since her rape. She wears a loose, shapeless dress.

"People say that crying is therapeutic, but Doctor, I'm sick of weeping. My husband has been great, you know, but I think he's getting impatient with my mood swings, ever since the- - - I know I need to say it- - - since my rape. What an ugly word." She dabs the corners of her swollen, olive-green eyes.

"When you sit in that chair, Emily, you don't

have to apologize for your feelings."

"I know," Emily smiles as she straightens the arm covers.

"I was always a trusting person. My husband always told me I was too trusting of people, too naive. Now, it's difficult to trust. Something else the rapist took from me, huh, Doctor? I'm scared. He is still out there. It's hard for me to go grocery shopping without looking over my shoulder, afraid to see him, or maybe afraid not to see him. I want him caught, then maybe I can stop being so paralyzed with fear." Emily stares at the floor and is silent for minutes.

"What are you thinking, Emily?"

"About the homework assignment you gave. I was to write about the rape, my feelings, and how it changed my life. Then I was to read it to you in today's session." She unfolds several sheets of paper, hands shaking. "Well, here goes."

After reading, her tears pour and drop to her chest. She piles the used tissues on her lap, some falling on the chair's seat cushion.

"I know you wanted me to deal with the out-of-body experience I had that day. Depersonalization, you called it. I know I was raped, but it felt as if I was watching a horrible movie, and it was happening to someone else. Is that crazy, Doctor?"

"Emily, you were protecting yourself. You shut down so your mind did not fully process what was happening. You were not going crazy. Most rape victims report the same emotional experience. What you read to me, is the beginning of coping with your rape. In time you will be able to recognize how you emotionally survived, and value your strength, with the courage to go on with your life. You said something early in the session that I want to follow up on. Remember you said your husband always felt you were too trusting and too naive of people. Do you think or sense that your husband, in some way, holds you partially responsible for your assault? Even though he hasn't said that to you. Think about this and we will discuss it on your next appointment. O.K.?"

She seems startled at my question, but then looks at her delicate watch that contrasts with the ugly, still pink scars on her wrist, and asks, "Is my hour up?"

Standing, Emily stares at the chair, "You know, the only time I truly feel safe is when I sit in this chair." Reaching in her purse for another tissue, she reluctantly moves to the door.

***

Marty sits with a defiant posture, leaning forward, with legs wide apart and his work-swollen, banged-up hands on his knees.

"I'm only here because my attorney told me to come. I don't believe in shrinks. Me being here is bullshit. Let's get to it. I thought the girl was at least eighteen. I didn't know she was fifteen, she had the body of a woman, no lack of tits and ass with her." His laugh dies in the silence.

"Look Mister, I'm no pervert. I don't have sex with kids!"

"But isn't that exactly what happened, Marty?"

His lips twitch, he blinks excessively, and nostrils flare. His hands roam the seat cushion and find some moist tissues.

"Looks like you had a crybaby in here earlier. What was her problem? Her old man wouldn't buy her a new BMW?"

"What makes you think the person was a female?'

"Because that's what women do, cry about everything. Like that bitch crying statutory rape.

Man, she was in a bar, came up to me, put her hand on my leg, and whispered in my ear of how she could make me feel real good. So I didn't ask to see her driver's license. She was in a bar, I just figured she was eighteen. She wanted it and I gave her what she wanted. Sure, I like'em young, but I don't do kids. You understand that, Mister, I don't go around looking for kids. Yeah, I mess around on my old lady, but as long as I pay the bills, she doesn't give a damn."

"You have any children, Marty?"

With neck veins swollen, "Mister, I ain't going to talk to you about my children. They have nothing to do about why I'm here. You got that! Now you want me to take some tests, want to know if my mama breast-fed me too long? If not, that's all I'm going to say."

Silence

"Yeah, I see the wheels turning in your head, Mister. What a jerk, you're thinking. I wasn't lucky like you. I grew up poor, on the wrong side of the tracks, like your kind like to say. My old man was a drunk. He beat the crap out of everyone, and I mean my mama, too. So, I don't have no fancy diplomas on the wall, but I work hard. My family don't want for nothing."

Silence

"So you send whatever report you dream up to my lawyer. I don't have time to hang around your office. I got a construction site to get back to."

Rubbing his unshaven face, he smiles. "I did enjoy the air-conditioning and the real comfy chair. I'm sure there is someone in the waiting room that needs to see you more than I do. Sorry for the dirt I left in your chair."

Smiling, "See you around, Mister."

He leaves quickly, perhaps fearing more silence.

***

She is a frail looking girl, weighing no more than ninety pounds, with skin so translucent that the small blue veins on her hands look like the rivers on a map. Sonja's face is without eyebrows and lashes. She wears a baseball cap low on her head, covering all but a wisp of rigid, auburn hair that sticks out the back. She makes almost no impression on the chair cushion.

"Since this is our first session, why don't you tell me a little about yourself, Sonja?"

"Well I don't know where to start. You know I'm fifteen. Most people think I'm about twelve. That's cool with me. I'm not anxious to grow up, like most of my peers. Probably some significance in the way I feel about that, huh, Doctor?"

"That's a keen insight, Sonja."

"Yeah, I thought so, too. Anyway, my dermatologist sent me to you. He says I 'display trichotillomania.' What a strange word, but its kinda fun to say. Just sort of rolls off your tongue, doesn't it? I'm a bright girl, doctor, gifted program and all that, so it's really stupid of me to be pulling out my hair. Saw you look at what's left of my brows and lashes- - -yanked them out. I'll show you my head. Pretty gross, huh? Most of the time, I don't realize I'm doing it. I'll be watching T.V. or reading and it happens. It's worse when I feel nervous. It freaks out my parents."

"I couldn't help but noticing that when you spoke of your parents, you were smiling. What's the smile about, Sonja?"

"I think we're going to get along just fine, Doctor. I would have been disappointed if you missed the smile, or didn't say something about it. I guess I found something I do that they can't control- - - but unfortunately, I can't either."

"Continue, Sonja."

"My mom said to be sure to tell you that I also

pull out my pubic hairs. I can't believe I'm saying this to you."

This time her smile is real. The flush red color of her skin is also real. Sonja begins to pull hair from the back of her head, and they fall on the chair's head support. She looks so tiny in her chair.

Silence

"Am I afraid of my sexuality, Doctor?"

"Sonja, how do you express your sexuality?"

"I'm not sure I want to discuss that on the first session," as Sonja deposits more hair on the chair, and again, smiles.

Silence

"You know, you are not the first therapist I've seen. When I was about ten, I saw a psychologist for an obsessive-compulsive disorder. She thought I experienced some kind of trauma that I buried deep in my psyche. She thought I might have been sexually abused. I would remember that! I didn't see her for very long. My dad thought she was crazy," as both hands roam her head.

"Anything else you want to share today?"

"Only that I miss a lot of days at school. The kids all think I'm a psycho. You think you can put me on home school?" She bats her absent eyelashes and smiles again.

Silence

"We will discuss that later in a future session. Our time is just about up."

She stands up, and retrieves her cap off the floor. She notices the hair on the graceful curve of the chair. She collects every hair, puts them in a tissue, then into her jean pocket.

She whispers, "I'm sorry," as if she is talking to no one, and exits without a good-bye.

***

Gathering up patient files, I turn off lamps and lock my file cabinet. At the door, I glance to survey my office. An interesting afternoon, but most days are equal in the outpouring of human suffering. Then, I notice an intriguing pattern of dim, muted light from the window. It cast itself only on the patient's chair, spotlighting it, like an actor on a dark stage. Tears, sweat, fear, panic, hate, dirt and hair are in the fabric. The chair absorbs so much of the patient's suffering- - - as I do. My role is to treat, but it is the chair that truly embraces. I lock my office door. The chair and I will be reunited tomorrow. And others will come to sit.

Notes

About the Author

Dr. John Morella, Ph.D., resides in Lafayette, Louisiana, in the heart of "Cajun Country."
Upon his retirement from a twenty-year practice of providing psychological services to the public, he wanted to rest and "smell the roses." However, as he looked back on his career in both his practice, and many years as an academic, he felt a need to write.
"A Guide for Effective Psychotherapy" was the result. He observed many patients struggle with understanding the process of psychotherapy, and believed a guide would benefit the consumer. He is currently working on a second book, with a working title, ***"Darn It, Give Teens a Break."*** Research supports that the vast majority of teenagers are psychologically healthy, and do not deserve the negative stereotypes perpetuated by the media and ourselves.

Printed in the United States
85769LV00003B/145-195/A

9 780977 820535